THE CENTURY PSYCHOLOGY SERIES

RICHARD M. ELLIOTT, *Editor*

THE EGO AND THE SELF

THE CENTURY PSYCHOLOGY SERIES

EDITED BY

RICHARD M. ELLIOTT, Ph.D., University of Minnesota

THE EGO AND THE SELF

Percival M. Symonds, *Ph.D.*

PROFESSOR OF EDUCATION
TEACHERS COLLEGE
COLUMBIA UNIVERSITY

New York

APPLETON-CENTURY-CROFTS, Inc.

PREFACE

Increasingly in recent years, the ego and the self have become reputable subjects for discussion and experimentation in psychology. There was a time when any psychologist who used these terms would be suspected of still believing in soul substance, would be classified as a mystic and would be challenged as unscientific. Today, ego and self are recognized as being naturalistic and as worthy of study and understanding as other, more concrete scientific psychological concepts. These terms have become common usage in the parlance of psychotherapy. And as the influence of the self on the results of psychological experiments has become recognized, it is fashionable today to test the "ego-involvement" of various situations.

This book defines the meaning of the several terms employed and presents systematically and in organized fashion the results of experimental findings and indications from clinical experience concerning the ego and the self. The book, therefore, becomes a text for those who wish to acquaint themselves with recent thinking and experimental work in this field. It is addressed principally to psychology students who are clinically oriented, but should serve as a basic text for any individual preparing himself for psychological counseling and psychotherapy, whether his preparation stems from psychology, psychiatry or social work. This book continues the series of my books elaborating principles of dynamic psychology which include *The Dynamics of Human Adjustment* and *The Dynamics of Parent-Child Relationships.*

As is explained in the text, the terms "ego" and "self" have been used because it is believed that there are two concepts which need separate terms in order to avoid confusion. *Ego* refers to the self as object—the self which perceives, thinks and acts—and which would be described by an outside observer. Used in this sense ego is, to all intents and purposes, identical with the ego as used in psychoanalytical literature. The ego is the objective self as it might be observed by a behaviorist. The *self,* on the other hand, is the subjective self as it is perceived, conceived, valued and responded to by the individual himself. The self is wholly subjective and corresponds to the "phenomenal self" described in the current phenomenological approach to the study of human nature. I am sure that Freud has never before been classed as a behaviorist; quite the opposite, he has been repeatedly challenged and criticized because he draws conclusions from evidence that is not reproducible. But Freud with his interest in understanding his patient as a functioning organism using whatever evidence he has access to about his patient and interpreting what his patient says to him seems quite the behaviorist as contrasted with those who profess the phenomenological point of view. Although Dr. Snygg assures me that he does not limit his evidence in studying an individual to the individual's introspective reports and indeed states in his book (with Combs), "Introspection is not a valid way of reconstructing the field, which can only be reconstructed from behavior," [1] when it comes right down to it, the only kind of evidence that these writers accept is that which comes from the individual being studied. "What the individual is seeking to preserve is not his physical self but the self of which he is

[1] Donald Snygg and H. W. Combs, *Individual Behavior.* New York: Harper and Brothers, 1949, p. 36.

aware, his phenomenal self." [2] So it seems necessary to use as evidence about an individual, both that which can be furnished by an outside observer and that which can be furnished by the individual himself, and for this reason two terms are employed—the ego and the self—to represent the objective and subjective aspects respectively.

It soon became apparent after *The Dynamics of Human Adjustment* was published that insufficient attention had been given to the rational and self-determining side of man, and in preparing the abridgement of that book in *Dynamic Psychology* this omission was remedied by the inclusion of a new chapter entitled "The Ego and the Self." However, only a portion of the material which was assembled at that time could be used for the chapter in *Dynamic Psychology,* and the total manuscript which was prepared has served as the basis for the present book. This new chapter in *Dynamic Psychology* has attracted considerable attention because it suggests "that it is possible, after all, for the organism to approach rationally many of his life problems." Korchin goes on to say, "What is now needed is a textbook that continues from where Symonds left off with consideration of the conditions under which growth and integration proceed, which places greater emphasis on ego and ego-ideal processes and which describes the growth of a mature conscience as well as an infantile superego." [3] With similar comments coming from many sources it seemed advisable to prepare this book from my larger manuscript which deals specifically with the rational and self-regarding side of man.

There is reason to believe that the current attention being devoted to the ego and the self is a healthy development for psychology. The ego is more than the independent operation

[2] op. cit., p. 56.
[3] S. J. Korchin, Review of *Dynamic Psychology* by Percival M. Symonds, Appleton-Century-Crofts, Inc., 1949, in *Journal of Abnormal and Social Psychology,* 44: 563–565, 1949.

of the processes of perceiving, thinking and acting. It is the organized and integrated action of these processes in the interests of adjustment. Indeed, the nature of the organization and integration of these processes is all-important. More could be said about each topic treated herein, but, in particular, more is going to be discovered about the complexity and variation in ego organization and integration. The most important thing about a man is how he marshalls his various forces and talents and applies them to the management of himself on the life around him. From the phenomenological point of view, the essence of a man is his concept and valuation of himself, and recent formulations would make the self concept and valuation the path of mental health.

The annotated bibliography of 211 titles with which the book closes is a rigorous selection from several hundred titles that were read and evaluated. The annotations, of course, represent my evaluation of the worth of each book or article, and I have attempted to present a précis of the contribution of each as a guide for the student who continues to explore any topic more fully.

Selected portions of the book served as the basis of a lecture delivered at the University of California at Berkeley in the spring of 1950.

P.M.S.

CONTENTS

THE EGO AND THE SELF

I

INTRODUCTION

The self is a topic in psychology which has been practically neglected in recent years and only now is beginning to find a reputable place in psychological discussions. Speculations with regard to the soul and the self have always been of interest to philosophers and to religious leaders. In this generation George H. Mead (145) has made the self a cornerstone for his philosophy of society. Among the psychologists William James (120) devoted a significant chapter to the self in his treatise on psychology. However, as psychology freed itself from the shackles of its philosophic origins and attempted to meet the demands of scientific method, it first gave attention to some of the elements of behavior, such as sensory perception, reaction time, and the like. Because so much of the groundwork is now laid, the time seems ripe for psychologists to devote attention to larger wholes.

Calkins (32, 33), writing in the first and second decades of this century, expressed the fear that psychologists, in their intense devotion to the study of isolated reactions in the interest of scientific accuracy, were losing sight of the individuals whose reactions they were studying, and she made a fervent plea for the scientific study of the self, but failed to go further in implementing her own position. Knight Dunlap (47) at one time made the same distinction between the ego and the self that will be made in this book, but he, too, failed to

1

elaborate this point of view, and his intense opposition to the possibility of unconscious processes prevented him from developing these concepts further.

In general, social psychologists have been the only group which has recognized the self and has given attention to it. At the beginning of the century Baldwin (14, 15) and Cooley (39) developed theories concerning the origin of the self. McDougall (143) found self-regarding tendencies to be among the most important of the sentiments. Gardner Murphy (149) and Kimball Young (211) have developed the concept of the self in their treatises on social psychology. But the main body of psychology has only recently recognized the self as a reputable topic for psychological research and inquiry. Gordon Allport's significant paper, "The Ego in Contemporary Psychology," created a new interest in the scientific study of the self (8). The work by Sherif and Cantril (191) on *The Psychology of Ego Involvements* indicates the growing strength of this interest.

Another line of thought concerning the self derives from Freud and the psychoanalysts. At the beginning of his work Freud was interested more in the details and elements of the mind, and it was only relatively late in his life that he recognized the part that the self plays in adjustment. Freud's term, *Das Ich,* has been translated into English as *ego,* and, stemming from psychoanalytical influence, the term is now widely used in current discussions of the self. Freud's little treatise on *The Ego and the Id* (83) stimulated discussion on the ego two decades ago, but within the last ten years another wave of papers from the psychoanalytic point of view integrates the ego psychology more thoroughly into the psychoanalytic system of thought.

Definitions

The distinction between the "I" and the "Me," between the subjective and objective meanings of the self, apparently was first made by Immanuel Kant (124). It was also later discussed by Schopenhauer (183). William James (120), probably drawing on this philosophical tradition, recognized two distinct concepts with regard to the self, which he called the "I" and the "Me." The "I" is the self as observer, or knower; the self that perceives the world about it and reacts to this world. The "Me," on the other hand, is the self as observed. The "I" can observe among many other things the "Me," that is, his own self, and the self can become an object of awareness and of value. Mead (145) maintained the same distinction between the "I" and the "Me" and elaborated these two concepts, stressing the social origin of the "Me."

Murphy (149) in his recent book *Personality* uses the two terms *"ego"* and *"self"* to stand for two phases of the self which do not, however, coincide exactly with those originally posited by James and Mead. Murphy refers to the self as the object of perception, whereas according to him the ego is a system of activities organized around the self to include both self-enhancement and self-defense. Jung (122) uses the ego to designate the conscious part of the personality while the self, including the ego, also embraces the unconscious to take into account the total personality. Bertocci (20), following Allport, uses *self* rather broadly to include much of personality, but uses *ego* to refer to the core of the self where the values are most intense. One hears it said of a person who feels that he has been neglected or depreciated with regard to something in which he excels that "his ego has been hurt." Guthrie and Edwards (101) in a recent book define the ego as "attitudes we hold toward our bodies, names, memories, and physical and mental traits." There is considerable confusion and inconsistency with regard to the use of the two terms *ego* and *self* in modern psychological writing.

In this book the two terms *ego* and *self* will continue to be used because it is believed that there are two concepts with regard to the self which correspond to the self as subject and as object which need to be kept distinct and which therefore require two different terms. *Ego* henceforth will be used to refer to that phase of personality which determines adjustments to the outside world in the interest of satisfying inner needs in those situations where choice and decision are involved. Or, to define the *ego* differently, it is an active process for developing and executing a plan of action for attaining satisfaction in response to inner drives. The *self*, on the other hand, refers to the body and mind and to bodily and mental processes as they are observed and reacted to by the individual. The ego as observer, thinker, and actor comes earlier in development than the self as observed. The self may have four different aspects. It may be the self as *perceived*, as, for instance, when one sees his physical self in the mirror or listens to his voice in a sound reproduction. Koffka (130), the Gestalt psychologist, was interested in the self as a figure on the ground or background of the total field of experience. Self from his point of view became one of the principal figures or configurations of perception to which the individual responds. The self may also be a *concept*. The little child thinks of himself as good or bad according to whether his father and mother call him good or bad. Thirdly, the self becomes of *value* and an *interest*. One may be curious about the self and the self may be cherished or despised. Fourthly, the self may be a *system of activities* in response to these values. The self is something to be enhanced or to be defended against attacks without, or even, on occasions, to be punished.

Snygg and Combs (192), who use the term *phenomenal*

self, state that it is the individual's own definition of his relations to the world about him. The phenomenal self is to all intents and purposes identical with self as used in this book. But as Frenkel-Brunswik (76) pointed out years ago, the ego may distort the self before it permits a percept of the self to emerge in consciousness. There may be a distortion into the opposite, as when a person believes he possesses traits which are the exact opposite of those recognized by his associates, or attempts to camouflage what he believes to be defects by diminishing or justifying them. Or a person may avoid facing the reality about the self by projecting his characteristics onto another person. The assertion by an individual of his guiding principles may actually be a compensation to cover up defects rather than a faithful representation of the actual possession of the virtues in question. As Frenkel-Brunswik adds: "We do not always know what we are, yet we do know in most cases what we need." Tendencies toward auto-illusion have been found to correlate with bad social adjustment.

Werner Wolff (209) reports experiments which indicate that the conscious evaluation of the self does not necessarily agree with the unconscious. He confronted individuals with photographs of their profiles, phonographic recordings of their voices, with samples of their handwriting mixed in with samples of the handwriting of others and other records of expressive movements. He found that individuals tended to overvalue or undervalue their own products, apparently in response to unconscious factors. When a form of expression was overvalued or overestimated the individual apparently acted in accord with his wish image; but when it was undervalued it was because there was a disparity between the self-ideal and the recognition that the actual expression fell short of this ideal and fear resulted from the tension caused by this disparity. Distortion of the self-concept should make one wary of accepting the phenomenological point of view too uncritically. In particular, one should not err, as did Rogers (173), in assuming that the statements that a person makes about himself represent all phases of the individual's perception, conception, and evaluation of himself.

2

THE STRUCTURE OF THE EGO

The ego has three distinct elements: one, perceiving (ego as the *knower*); two, thinking (ego as the *thinker*); and three, acting (ego as the *doer* or the *executive* or the *will*). In short, the ego first of all receives impressions from the outside world, then organizes these impressions so as to form a plan of action, and finally executes this plan in order to bring about desired satisfactions.

Perceiving

The first element of the ego is to receive impressions from the environment. The first perceptions in infancy are perceptions of inner need, but these perceptions are faint and blurred. The infant becomes sensitive to his hunger needs and when hunger is satisfied, to his need for sleep. These needs are experienced as inner tensions. Following the perception of these inner needs is the perception of outer conditions, particularly objects which may serve for the satisfaction of inner needs. One of the first objects to be perceived by the infant is the mother whom he recognizes in the first months as the source of supplies which can reduce inner tensions.

The world for the infant is perceived as either a source of satisfaction or as a threat of danger, and all perceptions may be thought of as having this dynamic significance. Perception is essentially an active process. It is something that the individual does rather than something that is done to him. Perception is a groping forward, a sampling of external stimuli to anticipate what can be expected from them on the basis of past experience. The most primitive form of perception is the taking in of food through the mouth. Later, as discrimination develops, this takes the form of tasting by which some objects are judged to be satisfying and others are judged to be repulsive, useless, or harmful. Perception as an active process is stimulated rhythmically by the periodic rise and fall of inner needs.

It is believed that the first perceptive stimuli are kinesthetic and proprioceptive, that is, stimuli which originate within the body and serve as signals of inner bodily states, positions, and movements (59). Many perceptions are more the body's response to an object than direct response to the object itself—at least the two are frequently simultaneous and it is difficult to distinguish between perception of the response and perception of the external object itself. The mouth has already been mentioned as one avenue of information concerning the outside world and one that the infant uses extensively during the second half of the first year. The eyes become the principal avenue of perception as soon as control of the eyes is developed, and throughout life in the normal person serve as his principal means of information concerning the world about him. Hearing is second in importance to vision. Finally the child learns to know objects by touch, by handling them, by manipulating them, and even by estimating size and distance by his locomotion.

The first perceptions are large in extent rather than small and detailed. They are all-enveloping, inexact wholes which only later can be differentiated into their parts. To the infant the world as perceived is big, confused, undifferentiated. The process of development in the early years is largely one of differentiation of perceptions.

Perception implies psychological distance from the data to be perceived. As long as an infant has his mother as the source of his supplies he has no need to be sensitive to his surroundings. Perception is stimulated by separation and the need to explore and inquire in order to locate the objects which may satisfy.

Memory traces are the remnants of perception (59). One writer has referred to the ego as the record of past object choices. In other words, as perceptions differentiate and multiply, the ego builds a store of experiences which serve him more and more adequately for making satisfying responses.

Under the category of perceiving must also be included *feeling* as an important ingredient in the total process of responding to the world about us. Feeling gives tone to our perceptions and helps us to evaluate our world. Experiences which arouse pleasurable feelings are reacted to as hospitable and kindly, to be accepted and encouraged, and even sought after. On the other hand, experiences which carry negative or unpleasant feeling we recognize as unfriendly and dangerous and we react to them by denial, refusal, and revulsion. Feeling should always accompany perceptions if they are to be caught up into the ego and integrated into the total process of adjustment. Cold, passionless perception and understanding represents a divorce of these processes from the ego. It is for this reason that mere intellectual understanding is ineffective in promoting therapeutic changes.

Although perception is primarily at the service of the ego in its main task of adaptation, perception may be valued independently as a source of pleasure. Every child enjoys novel and stimulating sights, sounds and tastes, and curiosity which stimulates exploration is motivated by the pleasure which the new experiences evoke.

Thinking

The second stage of the ego process consists in the working over of material perceived and preparing it as a program of action. Some writers believe that the *symbolic* processes which constitute thinking are the essence and core of the ego and that intelligence is the principal instrument with which the ego operates (43). The ego *relates* incoming stimuli to previous experience, a process which is known as apperception. This process of apperception, however, also has its dynamic significance, for the process of relating incoming impressions to previous experience has for its purpose deciding whether these new impressions carry the possibilities of providing frustration or satisfaction and of creating tension or relaxation. A second stage is the *selecting, sifting,* and *choosing* among incoming stimuli and memories and the impulses which they arouse. This involves anticipating in fantasy what might occur on the basis of previous experience to serve as a guide for future situations. In the mature person this is known as the weighing of issues. A third step is the *arranging* and *organizing* of these stimuli and impulses. Fourthly, these stimuli and impulses are *recorded* as more or less permanent memory impressions so that on a later occasion they can be recalled and again be considered among others for their possible values. Memory serves as a substructure for the ego and is a factor in helping the ego to achieve integration. The fifth and last step is that of *achieving a solution, planning,* and *making a decision* which can be carried into action. These various phases of thinking are functions of judgment and intelligence and the individual will be adequate in this phase of his ego to the extent that he has sufficient maturity and intelligence and provided his emotions do not interfere.

Thinking can be divided into two types: one which is directed largely by the drives, wishes, and anxieties with considerable pressure for the solution of the problem and the resolution of the difficulty; and the other in which there is less pressure from drives and anxieties, and which permits the individual to approach situations more objectively and with greater deliberation. In the first type, thinking is apt to be distorted and impulsive. In the second, where the pressure is less pronounced, it can represent a more adequate appraisal of reality. Naturally these two types blend into one another. An example of the first type of emergency thinking would be that of the adolescent girl who has the problem of yielding to her wild desire to join with friends in a late party or of following the advice of her mother who prudently suggests that she come in at an early hour. Planning leisurely during the winter months how one will spend his summer vacation is an example of the latter type of thinking.

Thinking, too, although primarily in the service of adaptation to reality, is pleasurable on its own account. Witness the pleasure that individuals find in solving puzzles or in quiz programs, where no basic needs are being served.

Acting

A third phase of the ego is to discharge its plans and impulses into action. Actually the primitive and archaic ego of the infant is largely concerned with gaining immediate satisfactions and manipulating its surroundings so that satisfactions can be achieved without delay. The ego is aided in this executive phase by two important functions in development —*manual grasping,* which develops during the first year and serves throughout life as a prime method of execution (19), and *locomotion,* which enables the individual to get about in space and thereby to bring himself in contact with objects and persons at a distance and thus to enhance his powers of control. Exploring and mastering the outside world involves aggressive behavior, but aggression which is sublimated into energetic action where the goal is the establishment of effective relations with others rather than the attainment of selfish pleasure.

However, the ego in its reactive phase has another important function, namely that of self-control and of binding action. If action is to be intelligent and planned, it cannot be too impulsive or immediate. There must be a time interval between the perception and response to it during which the thinking process can take place. This involves a postponement of action so that one phase of the acting ego is concerned with restriction, regulation, and direction of behavior. Only the ego can express a negative—there is no negative in the basic impulses and drives. Strict ego control, therefore, actually restricts the free expression of impulses. It is a sign of mature ego development to be able to wait and postpone action in the interest of more thoughtful and better planned action.

Acting also has its pleasurable side and, whereas behavior is primarily an ego function leading to better adaptation in the interests of gaining satisfaction, acting is also pleasurable on its own account. One has only to observe the young child running and jumping to realize that action brings pleasure. Rebellion against parents, teachers, and society, when a child is frustrated, may be as great a source of pleasure as the gratification of his basic needs.

Coördination of Ego Functions

The ego, however, is more than perceiving and feeling, thinking and acting, each considered separately. It involves the coördination of these functions into a smoothly acting mechanism. The psychoanalysts are fond of emphasizing that the ego derives its energy from the basic drives. The basic drives with their pain and discomfort egg the ego on and force it to find some object which can be used to alleviate the distress.

It is also important to note that the three phases of the ego must work together. The executive function depends on perception. Perception by itself cannot direct action but must depend upon the mediation of the thinking process. There is a possibility that consciousness is an important factor in helping to bind together and coördinate the several functions of the ego.

Jung (123: p 143) likened the ego to the general of an army. Alexander (6) went a step further and elaborated a helpful analogy between the relation of the ego to the rest of the personality and government. According to him the healthy ego is like a democratic organization. In the healthy personality the various forces in the personality—the basic driving forces, the demands, expectations, and restraints of society, at first external, later made part of the personality in a superego formation, and the planning, thinking, and deciding functions—all may express their demands and have them listened to. In other words there are no unconscious and repressed tendencies. And, as in a democracy, reconciliations between conflicting interests and demands are mediated by compromise, trading, and concession. The neurotic ego on the other hand represents an autocratic organization. Since a stern hand is laid on certain personality functions through repression, there is impoverishment in initiative, rigidity in adjustment, and control by anxiety and coercion. The neurotic ego represents an unhappy and unstable arrangement of the forces within the personality. Unlike so many analogies this one shows considerable fidelity of relation to the actual variations in the coördination of ego functions.

Mastery

The ego strives to achieve mastery over its surroundings. Two kinds of mastery can be recognized which may be called *passive* and *active* mastery, respectively. The infant under six months must depend upon his passive mastery, that is, his ability to bring to his succor parents and others who are responsible for his care. Crying is the young infant's principal resource which causes others to relieve his distress. Probably the infant's cry is one of the most intolerable of sounds, for it has a particularly rasping and penetrating quality which few people can endure. Nature has provided the infant with this resource which most adults feel impelled to relieve not only because of the sound itself but because of the image that it arouses of an infant in distress. In the last half of the first year an infant begins to develop methods for a more active type of mastery which involves the substitution of action for merely discharge reactions. Purposeful action then begins to take the place of impulsive action and passive mastery. As ability to foresee dangers and methods of warding off or avoiding them develop, the infant begins to find ways of protecting himself and achieving his own satisfactions.

Active mastery involves three elements. First there is the interpolation of a time period between the arousal of a desire or the perception of danger and the action which is to follow. The need for immediate gratification or escape from danger is incompatible with accurate judgment based on careful consideration of elements in the situation and postponement of the reaction. The person who is most likely to save himself in a catastrophe, such as a fire in a theatre, is the individual who has such self-control that he can momentarily postpone action to look around for the most favorable exit. The person who is likely to be the victim of circumstances is the one who rushes blindly and impulsively for the nearest exit. A second factor in active mastery is the ability to tolerate tension. The young infant is intolerant of tension and demands relief immediately. It is a sign of growing maturity when ability to tolerate tension begins to appear. A third factor in active mastery is the ability to bind primitive impulses by counter tendencies. The person who can substitute kindness in place of hostility is not only thereby able to control his hostility but has substituted in its place a form of behavior with advantageous social outcomes.

The functions of the mouth in taking in food and in tasting, of the hands in grasping, and of the legs for locomotion have already been mentioned. The eyes and speech also play important rôles in mastery. Two individuals in social situations may strive to assert mastery over one another by their gaze, and the less dominant person may admit the superiority of the other person by lowering his eyes. In our society, cleanliness and control of the excretory functions also occupy an important rôle in mastery. Just as a person learns to control his own excretory functions with regard to time and place so he later learns to order his environment and achieves mastery by developing system and efficiency. When active mastery fails there is a tendency to fall back on passive and receptive mastery. The person who has lost out in the struggle for existence will become a beggar or a mendicant and will look to society to provide him with the necessities and comforts of living.

Mastery or control also has its own pleasure values. Mastery produces a feeling of triumph and leads to the outward expression of this feeling following the lowering of tension which is an outcome of mastery. A child will give a whoop of delight when he wins the game. Many of the heroic efforts in which men and women engage may be directed toward the pleasure which results from the reduction of tension as mastery is achieved. We laugh when we feel confident of mastery even though there is still a tinge of anxiety at the possibility of failure. The greatest satisfaction comes in overcoming difficulties when the dangers which were missed can also be seen. The skier feels triumph, not only in having run the course, but also in the satisfaction of having successfully maneuvered the obstacles of the course.

Some Fundamental Considerations

EGO PROCESSES INSTEAD OF "THE EGO"

There is a danger in reifying the ego and in setting it up as something with more concreteness than it actually possesses. Some writers have suggested referring to ego processes rather than to such an abstraction as the ego. This is an important qualification. We know of no entity existing by itself such as the ego. All that is known is the process of perceiving, thinking, and acting. It is the integrated operation of these processes which constitutes the ego. Although "the ego" is a term used throughout this book, the reader should realize that it refers to "ego processes."

Much of Western thinking has its beginnings in Greek philosophy, and the still not uncommon notion that the soul somehow is a substance probably stems from Aristotle's insistence that everything is either a substance or an attribute of a substance. Descartes in more modern times helped to perpetuate this point of view by positing two kinds of substances—the corporeal and the incorporeal, the latter being spirit or soul and having an existence apart from the body. Indeed, Descartes went so far as to attempt to locate the soul in a particular part of the brain. This point of view is well illustrated by the first bequest commonly made in wills a century ago. For instance, the first bequest in a will probated in Virginia in 1799 read as follows: "I commend my soul to God that gave it, and my body to the earth to be buried at the discretion of my executors." [1] The first revolt from this point of view was made by the English philosopher, David Hume (117), who stated his position as follows:

There are some philosophers who imagine we are every moment intimately conscious of what we call our SELF; that we feel its ex-

[1] Quoted with the permission of Mrs. S. R. Powers from a will in her possession.

istence and its continuance in existence, and are certain, beyond the evidence of a demonstration, both of its perfect identity and simplicity. . . . For my part, when I enter most intimately into what I call *myself*, I always stumble on some particular perception or other, of heat or cold, light or shade, love or hatred, pain or pleasure. I never can catch *myself* at any time without a perception, and never can observe anything but the perception. When my perceptions are removed for any time, as by sound sleep, so long am I insensible of myself, and may truly be said not to exist. And were all my perceptions removed by death, and could I neither think, nor feel, nor see, nor love, nor hate after the dissolution of my body, I should be entirely annihilated, nor do I conceive what is farther requisite to make me a perfect nonentity. If any one, upon serious and unprejudiced reflection, thinks he has a different notion of *himself*, I must confess I can no longer reason with him. All I can allow him is, that he may be in the right as well as I, and that we are essentially different in this particular. He may, perhaps, perceive something simple and continued, which he calls *himself;* though I am certain there is no such principle in me.

However, today Hume's position seems to be entirely too atomistic. Hume destroyed more than he was justified in destroying by this extreme position, for our very language using "I" and "Me" signifies the recognition of an entity which can be identified, over and above the separate elements that are perceived. On this point another philosopher and psychologist, Mary W. Calkins (31: p. 227) made the following statement:

If, as Hume contends, there were no self,—if the word "self" were merely a name for a succession of ideas,—then one idea never could be looked upon as identical with another which had gone before; and no one even could say, "This is the same view, or bird note, or conclusion." For today's landscape, or sound, or reflection is a different idea, a different experience, from yesterday's. Yet we do have the experience of identity—in other words, we do recognize; and the fact that identity may not be attributed to ideas leaves us but the one way to account for the existence of identity. The consciousness of identity is really, then, the consciousness of the one and original self.

EGO A PRODUCT OF DEVELOPMENT

It is generally accepted today that the ego is not instinctive in man. The ego is not present at birth and develops only as a product of experience and learning. There is widespread belief in the religions of the world in reincarnation or the existence of the soul before birth, and in immortality, or the existence of the soul, after death. But there is no scientific basis for the belief that man has an immortal soul, something that he possessed before birth and which will last as a separate entity after death.

EGO AND SELF IN ANIMALS

One question which is frequently raised is whether or not animals possess a self. This question perhaps should be separated into two parts: Do animals possess an ego as well as a self? It is doubtful whether even the highest primates below man possess an ego in the same sense that man does. However, some animals do possess ego processes. They do perceive, they certainly act, and they carry on rudimentary thought processes. However, none of these processes are developed as they are in man and certainly they are not integrated into a highly complex organization. In man adjustment is not entrusted to separate instincts acting more or less autonomously but is the function of an independent organization based primarily on his capacity to think. This function we are calling the ego.

It is even more certain that animals do not possess selves. In order to perceive one's own processes of adjustment and to conceptualize them it is necessary to be able to symbolize the processes, and there is no evidence that animals are capable of this symbolic process except in the most rudimentary way. Yerkes [2] states that no animal below man according to

[2] Personal communication from Dr. Yerkes. See also reference (210).

his observation, even including the primates which he had opportunity to observe personally, ever responds to the self in the mirror situation. A primate may be curious as to what he sees in the mirror, but there is no evidence that he refers back to himself what he sees.

CAPACITY OF EGO FOR DEVELOPMENT

Because the ego is a product of experience it is mutable and changeable (41, 77). Ego is something that has indefinite capacity for development. Although the ego has a beginning, there is no limit to the possibilities of its expansion and organization as it becomes modified through experience. Through expansion of the ego one can learn to comprehend more and more of the physical and social world about him; limited only by intellectual capacity one can learn to apply his expanding knowledge to the solution of problems which confront him, and limited only by the resources available one can learn to control and modify the environment to meet his needs. There is also no limit to the extent that the ego can expand its functions, thus making the individual more and more morally sensitive and responsible.

FORCES TO WHICH EGO IS RESPONSIVE

The ego is responsive to three separate forces (85). The first of these is the inner drives which serve as the original motivating force of the ego. The second is the external world which serves both as a source of frustration of drives and also the means of satisfying them. The third group of forces to which the ego is responsive is the superego and self-ideals, namely, those expectations of family and society which the ego has accepted as its own, more or less uncritically, in response to its fears of punishment on the one hand and of abandonment on the other.

Because the ego is responsive to these three forces it is also exposed to three sources of danger which may threaten its strength and expose it to weakness. In the first place, the ego is threatened by the strength of the basic drives. These may be overwhelming in their demands and may threaten the effectiveness of the thought processes which cannot function successfully under extreme pressure. When the drives are urgent, action is likely to be impulsive and of an emergency nature. When the urgency of drives is reduced in later childhood a child can view and study his world more objectively and can establish more objective criteria for meeting his problems. But as the sexual and aggressive drives become more powerful in adolescence the ego becomes again threatened and is forced to use various mechanisms of defense.

The second danger to which the ego is exposed is the external world which, too, is peremptory and impersonal in its demands. For the infant these outer demands are the restrictions and expectations imposed by parents with their constant "Do's" and "Don't's" that either force the child into unwilling action or restrain him from the immediate satisfaction of his wishes. Little by little the child must learn that there has to be a time interval between the arousal of a wish and the fulfilment of a plan for achieving satisfaction of the wish. Every ego function has its disagreeable features, for postponement of action involves temporary frustration while decisions and plans are being made. The third danger which the ego faces is the demands of the superego, which may be even more strict and compelling than the demands of the outside world. The guilt and punishment which a child feels he deserves and fears for some minor infraction is frequently many times more intense and severe than that which his parents will administer.

Ego may be thought of as an organization of these elements of personality and its strength depends on the free interplay between them. The flexibility of the ego is restricted and it functions less effectively when any of the three sources of danger becomes too strong and compelling.

The ego cannot be conceived as a static, finished, perfected entity. The essence of the ego is that it shall be an adapting apparatus, constantly mediating between the needs of the organism and the demands of the environment. Ribot (169, 170) said many years ago that the ego exists only on condition of continually changing. As the ego serves its function of helping an individual adapt to circumstances and solve new problems, it consists of ever-changing series of conscious states. If ever ego processes become static and repetitive they would fail in their task of helping an individual adjust to the constantly changing inner demands of his organism or to the changing conditions of the outside world.

EGO AND SELF AND CONSCIOUSNESS

The extent to which the ego and the self are conscious processes is a question of perennial interest. Ego processes may take place at the unconscious, the preconscious, and the conscious level; however, they are essentially conscious phenomena. These processes involve the solution of difficulties and the resolution of conflicts which take place consciously. Consciousness has a limiting and directing function but does not play an important initiating rôle (96). Many ego functions, however, are unconscious. Not only may perception and action take place unconsciously, but even thinking may proceed without the intervention of consciousness. The familiar phenomenon of solving problems during one's sleep would indicate that the re-structuring of thought elements may take place without the aid of consciousness. The repressing forces operate to a large extent unconsciously, for we are usually not aware of inner forces which repress and inhibit our activities. The ego knows nothing of successful repressions or of reaction formations, and indeed it exercises some resistance to having these brought to consciousness because the functions repressed may be in themselves dangerous and painful.

The self, on the other hand, is usually conscious. If we think of the self as the individual's awareness of his own ego processes it becomes clear that as this awareness grows in distinctness, it functions more fully on the conscious level. On the other hand, many of the activities of the ego, particularly in enhancing and protecting the self, may operate unconsciously. Few individuals are aware of the extent to which they may be compensating for inferiority or projecting or rationalizing to protect some of their unacceptable motives. Jung (123: p. 83) repeatedly emphasizes that the self comprehends only a small part of the ego. There are many ego processes which the self never knows and of which it is never aware. "What the self comprehends is perhaps the least part of that which complete consciousness would include within itself." [3]

Brierley (26), a British psychoanalyst, devotes a long paper to a consideration of the goals of life in the light of modern conditions. She concludes that man needs as wide a grasp on reality as it is possible to achieve so that each person may make reasoned choices and decisions. She is particularly afraid that man will not take into account his own inner nature, particularly its unconscious roots. She stresses again and again that the conscious part of the ego is by no means the whole personality but only the conscious agent of the total personality. This assumption that only what we are aware of about ourselves matters leads to a confusion between the basic aims of living and the means and consequences of adaptation, between pleasure-pain and other affective indices of the consequences of action and the basic aims and goals of life as expressed in our fundamental drives. She also stresses that

[3] In this quotation the word *self* has been substituted for Jung's term *ego* to make the statement consistent with the usage in this book.

whereas the ego concerns itself with objects and persons as such, it tends to forget that the significance of objects and persons is dependent upon the relations established with them. Her plea is that each individual be helped to know himself better, his unconscious tendencies as well as those of which he is aware, so that he may arrive at integrative, practicable decisions.

EGO AND THE FUTURE

The ego is primarily concerned with the future (8). It is one aspect of personality which is concerned with planning action and anticipating the effects of action. Goals and values depend upon the development of the ego.

RELATION OF EGO TO BASIC NEEDS AND DRIVES

Some writers have thought that the ego is an antagonist to the basic needs of an individual because one of the functions of the ego is to postpone action in favor of deliberation. However, the ego is not necessarily hostile to the basic drives (59). As a matter of fact, the ego develops originally to serve the basic drives and to help toward reducing their strength in the interests of satisfaction. If the ego appears to be hostile to the basic drives and to dampen the possibility of pleasure, this is a result of special learning. Part of this learning may be thought of as the result of natural consequences, as when an individual learns that impulsive action will frequently result in pain as well as in pleasure. Equally important as the learning from natural consequences is the learning that takes place through education, that is, the restrictions imposed by parents and society, and the punishment that follows breaking rules. If the ego appears to be forgetful of the individual's basic desires it may indicate that there is an abandonment of immediate pleasure in favor of more comprehensive satisfactions in the long run.

Infrequently the ego may repress the basic desires in response to family and social pressures and demands. Maximum need-satisfaction cannot be thought of narrowly in terms of inhibition in response to family and social demands or freedom from these demands. Satisfaction is also a function of the concept of the self. A person who is comfortable and effective with himself, who has not found it necessary to repress his recognition of inner impulses or outer environmental demands, who feels adequate to the demands placed upon him and who is under a minimum of tension is the more likely to derive satisfaction from the experiences of life than the person who is at war with himself, who is under tension, and who feels inadequate.

RELATION OF EGO TO MORALS AND CHARACTER

Initially the ego cannot be said to have moral tendencies. Basically the ego is neither egoistic nor altruistic, coöperative or competitive. But these directional tendencies start early in life, are fostered by the influences exerted by parents and the wider community and are stimulated by one's own self-ideals. Since the self early becomes a central value it is only natural that egoistic tendencies should also receive an early incentive. Altruistic tendencies depend upon patterns set by the family and the culture in general. Ego tendencies toward competition or coöperation also take the direction which the family structure suggests and this in turn is in part influenced by tendencies in the community at large.

Character has been defined by Fenichel (59) as the ego's habitual mode of adjustment. As the ego takes on its pattern of perceiving, thinking, and acting, and as it adopts special stratagems for mastery and becomes more or less controlling and repressing, fixed patterns of adjustment take form, and these are what is known as character.

3

FUNCTIONS OF THE EGO

Basically, the ego has two main functions—namely, to satisfy wishes and to avoid dangers. The better the ego development, the better the chances of gratifying desires and of using the outside world to fulfill wishes. Of the dangers that the ego seeks to avoid, certain ones come from the outside environment, while others come from within. The ego avoids traumatic situations, that is, those which contain stimuli of overwhelming intensity in which the usual modes of adjustment fail and to which an abrupt change in previous adaptation must be made. But the ego avoids inner dangers, that is, possible frustrations of inner wants and needs.

More specifically, the ego is recognized as possessing four distinct functions: 1) reality testing, 2) a synthetic function, 3) a repressing and inhibitory function, and 4) the building of memories (78).

Reality Testing

The ego tries out reality in its search for adaptation. Reality testing from this point of view is the basis of thinking. Different persons see reality differently, as is well known when one compares his own experiences with those of another person. Some persons are more responsive to color and form while others are more responsive to relationships. It is interesting to note what different people observe when they enter a new room. Some are sensitive to the color scheme and the decorative features. Others note the objects of interest; still others are sensitive to imperfections, irregularities, and blemishes. Each individual has his own mode of perceiving the reality about him. One function of the ego is to keep contact with objects which might prevent gratification on the one hand or which might provide gratification on the other.

A feature of reality testing is that of sampling situations in small quantities in anticipation of entering completely and realistically into the situation itself. One may approach a strange food by tasting a very little of it in order to ascertain whether one wants to eat it in larger quantities. A child may engage in rough play with his parents in order to see if in a miniature and playful situation the danger which he fears when parents threaten punishment will be really formidable and overwhelming.

Reality testing also means sampling in fantasy the anticipation of experience. As one approaches a red light in an emergency dash to the hospital various alternatives flash through the mind. On the one hand one envisages a traffic summons, an accident to another car, an injury to a pedestrian. On the other hand he sees a chance of saving a precious second (and life). Fantasy, therefore, has a valuable function in normal development, for it provides a method by which alternatives can be tested out without undergoing all of the dangers involved.

When reality becomes too unbearable there may be a retreat to fantasy. In adult life fantasy and reality must be kept in some form of adjustment. Fantasy cannot depart too widely from reality or adjustment will become unreal and ineffective. Children, however, because so much of their experience lies ahead of them, do not feel restricted by the necessity of making fantasy and reality agree. Children are not criticized when their fantasy world becomes quite distorted, for it is recognized that it is necessary for them to go through some sort of exploratory experience as a preparation for meeting the experiences of real life. However, even the child who develops a rich fantasy life, if he is normal, differentiates between fantasy and reality. Enjoying the desired aim in fantasy is a way the normal person solves the problem of waiting. Rather then endure unrelieved frustration he receives a partial gratification to his postponed satisfactions through anticipation in fantasy.

Reality testing involves sampling actively what one might at another time experience passively. A little girl coming home from the dentist was found to be playing the rôle of dentist with her younger brother. In this play she was living through again in an active rôle the experiences which she had to undergo passively as a sufferer in the dentist's chair. By working through these experiences in play she became better able to tolerate them on another occasion and was less frightened by what she was about to experience.

A fourth feature of reality testing is repetition. The writer recently enjoyed reading aloud to a four-year-old boy the story of the red fire engine, a book the child had recently received as a gift. This story was the epic of a fire engine which answered the fire alarm and contributed to putting out the fire. Pictures showed the engine racing to the scene of the fire, the flames devouring part of the house, the family that had moved the furniture out into the yard. At the conclusion of the story the child said, "Read it to me again." The child was as absorbed in the story the second time as much as the first and was unwilling to have any incident in the story abridged or omitted. The writer was not aware at first of the extent to which this story was exciting and anxiety-provoking nor the extent to which the child felt a need of having it read to him again in order that he might master some of the elements of danger which it had for him.

MOTIVATION OF REALITY TESTING

There are at least four motives for reality testing. In the first place, the child uses reality testing in order to determine to what extent his image of the world has been distorted. Fantasies produced under the stress of intense need and anxiety may produce images of the world which depart far from reality. The child is constantly testing out the people around him in order to see whether they have the fierceness or the kindness which he fears or hopes for. Institutionalized children not infrequently run away to their own homes in order to test whether someone at home may really after all love them.

Secondly, a child is continually testing for the presence of objects (or persons) once temporarily lost and which he fears he may lose again. A little child may call out after he has gone to bed to make sure that his parents are in the next room and have not gone out to the movies, or he may even demand that the light be left on in the hallway or in his room as a reassurance that he is not completely deserted in the darkness. Not only does he test for the presence of objects but also for their pleasure-giving qualities. Little children may tease adults for the privilege of going to the circus or for the penny to put in the slot machine, not only to obtain these pleasures but also to test out the willingness of the adults to give to them.

Thirdly, there is continual testing in childhood for the presence of danger. A child tries out the people and situations about him to determine the extent of external danger and whether this danger can be borne. Children are continually provoking their elders, both parents and teachers, in order to see how far they can go before their wrath is aroused and punishment administered. There is also a need to determine how serious the punishment will be and whether it can be tolerated. The child who apparently willfully annoys when he is certain that punishment will be forthcoming in many instances may be provoking the punishment in order to test its severity. Affects such as anxiety or shame are part of the reality testing function. They serve as signals to warn of the presence of danger and to put the individual on guard in order to make preparation for it.

A fourth motive for reality testing is to try out the strength of one's inner demands in order to determine whether they too can be tolerated. A child may place himself in the way of temptation in order to try out the strength of his wishes and to determine whether they become too dangerous in the light of his own conscience and scruples. A boy may try increasingly high dives in order to see whether he can tolerate and survive the impact with the water and acquire the necessary skill and control. A man may try out some new and potent liquor to see whether he can "hold it."

One result of reality testing is the development of the capacity for discrimination. The baby puts everything into his mouth without discrimination. Later, however, there is a tendency to taste and to either choose or reject as discrimination develops. Therefore many children's activities are in the form of dares or trials so that they can discriminate between those experiences which do or do not yield pleasure and those which are or are not dangerous.

Building the ability to tolerate tension, which has previously been discussed, and building the ability to judge reality are two aspects of the same thing. They both involve a trial, a testing in small amounts and tentatively postponing the major satisfaction or withdrawing until one is sure of the way.

Reality testing not only uses the affects but actually changes the ego's relation to them. Reality testing tends to reduce the intensity of anxiety, guilt, and shame. As the situation is tried out and found to be less dangerous than it was believed to be in fantasy, the need for anxiety is reduced. The better acquainted a person is with the real world about him, the better he understands the people and the forces which control his world, the less need he has for anxiety.

Many neurotic solutions to problems, on the other hand, tend to destroy the effects of reality testing and to negate its influence. For instance, the neurotic need of satisfying an ideal may benumb the critical judgment of the ego. When a parent or a teacher punishes a child because he believes that what he is doing is best for the child he is giving over his capacity to judge the situation critically in the service of his somewhat stubborn and blind ideals. Reality testing makes use of the utmost capacities of an individual for critical and differential appraisal of the situation and is the opposite of the fixed rule and the blind and obsessional method of meeting the new situation.

PLAY AND REALITY TESTING

Play in childhood is an attempt to assimilate a process more completely by anticipating and reviewing it and thereby gaining mastery over it (203). Play in childhood meets all the criteria of reality testing which have been discussed. It is a trying out in fantasy and in anticipation what may be experienced in reality at a later time. Play involves sampling in small quantities. It is an active trying out of a situation which later and in reality the person may experience passively. Play involves the attempt to gain mastery over one's own body and its processes as well as over persons and things in the outside world. Child analysts have demonstrated that as a little child is playing with water and sand, with the toy pistol and the ball, or with the doll and doll house, he is in fantasy projecting his own bodily functions into the outside world and is attempting in this symbolic fashion to understand them better and to gain mastery over them. But at the same time

he is anticipating the situations that he sees his elders experiencing and even far in advance he is trying them out in
order to test how they feel and whether he can master the
intensity of feeling which they seem to hold for him.

Play for a child is a temporary absence from reality (203).
A mother may have to call her son away from his fantasies to
the necessity of changing his clothes, eating a meal, or going
to bed. These latter represent the realities of living as contrasted with the play, which is the fantasy life and testing of
reality. Play also represents a temporary departure from the
demands of the superego. In play a child can take on the
character of the bandit, the desperado, the gangster, the gun-
man, or the clown, none of which, normally, he would permit
himself in real life.

Synthetic Functions of the Ego

A second main function of the ego is to harmonize the different elements in the personality and to help the personality
operate smoothly and effectively. As was stated on p. 19, the
ego may be looked upon as the servant of three forces: 1) the
inner needs striving for satisfaction and the basic drives striving for expression, 2) the outer world with its demands in
the form of social expectations and restraints, and 3) the superego or the inner representation of these demands and expectations of the outer world. A well-integrated ego implies that
a person has good ego-control instead of being impulsive,
that he is able to concentrate his energies on tasks before him
instead of scattering his efforts in aimless or destructive behavior; that he is able to harmonize his wishes and needs with
those of individuals with whom he associates instead of being
selfish and egocentric; that he is able to pursue his objectives
to a satisfactory termination; that he is not too easily disorganized and is able to tolerate frustration.

There are a number of reconciliations between possible

warring factions in the personality for which the ego is responsible. In the first place, the ego is responsible for reconciling wishes and drives with the demands of outer reality. On a rainy day it may be unwise to go to the game, and one must learn the necessity for giving up a pleasure at the insistence of outer circumstances as wisdom dictates.

Secondly, the ego has the responsibility of reconciling its wishes and drives with superego demands. The deprived youngster who sees the toys and sweets in the five- and ten-cent store is tempted to take what does not belong to him, but these impulses are countered by the teachings of his parents, church, and school, which say it is wrong to steal. Some form of reconciliation must be made between these two warring demands.

In the third place, it is necessary to reconcile the superego with the demands of outer reality which may have changed from the demands which helped to establish the superego in the first place. A young woman accepted the dictates of a strict evangelical sect and gave up many pleasures. As the years passed, however, she found that she was thereby ostracizing herself from friends and was becoming more and more isolated. The conflict became increasingly intense as the need to yield to the demands of real life about her became more pressing. Finally a reconciliation was effected through the help of a friend who pointed out to her that the demands of her religious sect were not those that were sanctioned by the Bible.

In the fourth place, the ego must help to reconcile differing impressions of immediate perception and memory of past experiences. Memory may become distorted and the dangers and frustrations of some previous situation may become exaggerated. The ego must keep alive the ability to judge each new situation afresh in spite of memory of unfortunate experiences in the past.

Fifth, to the ego is delegated the responsibility for reconciling inconsistent ego nuclei within. For instance, one part of the ego which may come from one parent finds an advantage in settling down in one community with a given job in order to make a success of that work. Another part of the ego, perhaps coming from the other parent, sees an advantage in traveling and its broadening influences. Here the ego again must reconcile these two conflicting nuclei within and make a decision which will harmonize these two competing trends.

Sixth, the ego has the responsibility for reconciling the painful past with a hopeful future. The ego must overcome the "burnt-child" tendency which forever avoids the scene of past failures or accidents. The ego has the task of discriminating between the features in past situations which led to failure or misfortune and those features in the future which may avoid these same failures or accidents.

Synthesis of the different parts of the personality is necessary for effective thinking. Conflicts of too great intensity absorb too much energy to permit an individual to pay attention to differential criteria in the situation about him. The child, for instance, who is torn between conflicts with regard to his home, who wishes to strike back aggressively to demanding parents but believes that this is wrong, is often unable to do his school work adequately. These conflicts may work themselves out in excessive fantasy or excessive repression or in a need for roundabout methods of punishing the parents. These neurotic solutions to the conflict prevent a child from devoting his attention to the activities about him and the result may be a failure to learn to read or to master other skills which it is the task of the school to provide. Effective thinking requires the capacity to see the problem as a whole. Any split in the personality, any conflict between elements of the personality is almost certain to block off certain aspects of the world about, prevent them from receiving due consideration, and hence may serve as an obstacle to effective thinking.

Repressive and Inhibitory Functions of the Ego

The third main function of the ego comprises its capacity to postpone action in favor of deliberation. Endurance of tension is a function of the ego. The various defense mechanisms are elementary features of the ego's attempts at the organization of the total personality. The defense mechanisms are the ego's primitive attempts to resolve conflicts and thereby to keep the personality functioning smoothly. The kind of defense adopted in later life is believed to be a repetition of the kind of solution arrived at in early danger situations. Spitz (193) has recently described a depression syndrome in infants in the sixth to the eleventh month who are deprived of their mothers over a considerable period of time. These infants show their depression by quiet weeping and withdrawal from contacts and sensitivity to those about them. Although he does not present the evidence, it would be reasonable to assume that this early method of meeting deprivation by depression sets a pattern which will be repeated in later life episodes in which the individual is deprived of the companionship of someone who is affectionally important. Another infant who is stimulated to strong aggressive responses by a weak, yielding, or punitive mother may likewise adopt aggressive solutions to difficulties in later life.

In infancy there is no real ego superiority over the drives. The repressive and inhibitory functions of the ego develop much later. The reason why these functions of the ego are slow in developing is in part because the push of wish-fulfillment is so strong in the infant and in part because alternate methods of gratification have not developed. The ability to repress and inhibit grows along with the capacity to find adequate methods of gratification.

One function of the ego is to build an apparatus of non-discharge. To inhibit an activity requires the mobilizing of energy for mastering overwhelming excitation which must be brought under control. There are two reasons for developing these controlling functions. There is the danger of being overwhelmed by external dangers on the one hand, (such as the demands and threats of punishment from parents) and by the pain from overwhelming unsatisfied internal demands and drives on the other hand. The reason the ego must find methods of defending itself against its inner drives is because it is not prepared to satisfy them. Were adequate modes of satisfaction available, the need for repressing them would not be so intense.

The capacity to shut off perception is an important phase of the repressing faculty. Sleep is a prototype of all later repressing capacities while fainting is another act which bears resemblance to repression. Freud (79) and Fenichel (59) use the term *countercathexis* to indicate those interests and behavioral trends which, by acting opposite to a tendency, help to master an unacceptable impulse. Countercathexis is perhaps best illustrated by a reaction formation which consists primarily in the concentration of mental energy in a given task and along one kind of response which prevents the opposite response from appearing. For instance, a person with strong drives to be taken care of may develop tendencies toward independence as a reaction formation against his dependency needs. His unwillingness to accept aid from others serves as a method of hiding from himself and others his strong wishes to become dependent.

The repressive functions of the ego to a certain extent make it less capable of mastering strong excitation when threatened.

All repression requires an expenditure of energy which may be a constant drain on the resources of an individual and in an emergency these counter tendencies may actually weaken the ego so that the person becomes overwhelmed by circumstances and by his drives. The individual who apparently has developed an ironclad character may be the one who will succumb most completely to adverse circumstances.

Accordingly, what has been repressed exists outside the ego and is unacceptable to the ego. For this reason impulses that have been warded off through repression impair an individual's capacity for reality testing. They preclude differential thinking and block the ego in its attempts completely to organize experience. Many individuals limp along half effectively and their adjustments could be measurably increased were their egos in contact with all phases of their personality. Sometimes the ego inhibits out of its strength, as a precautionary measure against unacceptable parts of the personality, but sometimes the ego represses on account of its weakness and impoverishment because it is not able to deal with the impulses in a more adequate fashion.

The ability to wait and tolerate tension is a function of the normal person. Some neurotics hold to the belief that to postpone gratification is a sign of weakness and damages their self-respect. They believe that the strong individual is the one who tolerates no hindrance to his pleasures. Actually, however, it is normal to be able to repress impulses in the interests of a more thoughtful solution to problems. To be able to control ourselves is as important a need for building and maintaining self-respect as is self-expression. Instead of hurting an individual's self-respect, control of impulses actually helps to build self-love and self-regard. It is the neurotic who holds the belief that it is harmful to deny gratification of the sexual urges because the strain which such denial entails actually does damage to the personality. But if the anxiety which surrounds sex can be drained off, then reasonable exercise of sexual functions is found to add to the individual's well-being because it contributes to his dignity and self-respect.

Building Memories

The fourth function of the ego is that of building up a store of memories as a basis for judging and deciding with regard to future situations. Memory is to a degree a disturbing function inasmuch as it is necessary to retain the painful as well as the pleasant. The ego, however, must tolerate these painful memories, for if they are not too frightening or disturbing they can serve the ego in its capacity for judging the implications of the situation ahead.

4

DEVELOPMENT OF THE EGO

Man is not born with an ego but the ego is the product of learning and development. Ego development begins at birth and is a continuous process which is never completed. It may be safely stated that every experience to which an infant or child responds with feeling contributes its small quota either positively or negatively to ego development.

Ego Development, a Process of Differentiation

In the beginning, the infant is not separated from his mother. The act of birth then may be considered the beginning of ego development, for in this traumatic act of separation the infant is forced to begin to perceive, think and act for himself. At the beginning of life, before the ego has developed, reactions to stimuli are undifferentiated. At first the ego includes too much. It does not differentiate between the self and the rest of the world. In times of stress or extreme fatigue there are always traces in every adult individual of this undifferentiated state, as he may appropriate articles that do not belong to him or importune others to satisfy his needs.

The ego grows out of separation and frustration. As the mother is sometimes absent, the infant is forced to look around for her presence and to reach out for her. The infant has to learn that the non-ego is that which may bring pain and frustration while the ego is that which can bring pleasure.

This process of differentiation is extremely gradual and it is not possible to locate it in any single episode. However, the process of weaning undoubtedly hastens differentiation and the development of the ego. Weaning which is too harsh and abrupt may have traumatic consequences and result in an ego which forever after shows tendencies toward overdependency in critical situations, but with the gradual deprivation of indulgences the infant can be helped to become reliant and secure. The young child needs guidance toward an independent emotional existence (194). At first the hands serve as a means of discharging tension at the mouth to be noted when a baby "mouths" his own fingers. Later with the coöperation of the eyes the hands serve as tools for controlling and modifying the outer world (112). Walking, too, as it makes possible locomotion toward and from objects, increases independence and accelerates the differentiation process. By retarding weaning or the development of walking the infant is forced to remain dependent and his ego development may be retarded. But an ego forced to function too early before its capacities have sufficiently developed may at the same time give rise to insecurity and anxiety.

It should not be thought that differentiation is solely a function of perception. The ego develops primarily in reaction. Many writers have emphasized the importance of motor release for ego growth. The child develops his ego to the extent that he is given opportunity to try things out for himself, to explore and gradually to learn methods of adaptation. The ego develops in the self-assertive responses of an active infant to other assertive individuals. And as the mother responds to the infant's self-assertion the infant learns to be concerned about his impulses. At first he simply cries and thrashes about, without regard to what happens as a result, but as he finds that others respond to his behavior he learns to be concerned about it and possibly to control and direct it.

Benedek (17) has proposed the concept of *confidence* as an important factor in the development of the ego. She refers to the feeling that develops in the infant when the mother temporarily leaves and he is assured she will soon return. The infant who has not experienced disappointment in this regard and feels assured that indulgence will follow a brief period of deprivation is the infant who will develop the capacity to tolerate deprivation. This building of confidence, which apparently is a real response on the part of the infant, protects the infant from fear of object loss. Normal babies show confidence when separated from the mother and achieve a certain stability of response. Infants who have been hurt through deprivation will fail to develop this attitude of confidence and consequently fail to develop a toleration of deprivation. Confidence is believed to be a factor in developing capacity to respond to reality and the ego develops more surely in those infants who have developed this capacity for confidence. As experience in child guidance accumulates, it becomes more and more clear that the presence or absence of the mother becomes increasingly important and significant in the development of personality.

Ego Development a Process of Integration

Early development must be thought of as a series of loosely related experiences. The infant learns separate reactions to such different situations as nursing, dressing, bathing, and fondling. He also learns reactions to different persons who make different demands on him and respond to his needs in different ways. In the very young child, consciousness is intermittent and discontinuous. Waking periods are broken by frequent naps, and the change from one activity to another lacks the continuity that it has at later ages. Winnicott (205) has added to our understanding of how the ego becomes integrated in early infancy. He believes that integration is achieved in part through the continuities of the surroundings. At first there is an integration of sleeping and waking states and only gradually is the waking state dissociated from sleeping. Bits of nursing experience, faces seen, sounds heard, smells smelt are only gradually pieced together into one being called mother. When a baby is kept warm, handled, bathed, nursed, and named by a single individual—the mother—he is helped to tie these experiences together. There is a linking together of inner experience with a continuity of outer reality. Winnicott sees a necessity for a certain amount of uniformity in the world for a baby to acquire a core of ego integration and he believes richness of experience should be added only to a base of consistency and monotony.

Some writers have referred to ego nuclei, that is, the variety of reactions that characterize early development (94). These different ego subsystems make it possible for the ego to be a member of many different "we-ness" groups. These different ego nuclei are to an extent autonomous and function independently of one another. The child responds in one way to mother, in another way to father, and in still another way to brothers and sisters. Later he responds to playmates, to nursery school teachers, to classmates in school. Each of these groups has different expectations and requires different responses. Not infrequently the child who is unruly and difficult at home becomes coöperative in the kindergarten. The child develops gradually out of a state of existing in psychic fragments to one of becoming a coherent entity. It is the first five or six years when the superego is being formed which seem to place the greatest strain on the ego's ability to integrate because of the persistent demands being placed on the child.

It is a characteristic of personality to attempt to achieve an integration of these reaction systems. One may well ask what it is that keeps the ego functioning in the interests of integration. Some present-day psychologists have referred to this process of integration as a natural and inevitable tendency of personality. Rogers (173) has made this tendency to seek consistency a cornerstone of his theory of psychotherapy, and Lecky (135) has written on self-consistency. This integration apparently takes form around some dominant goal or core of activity. Fodor (65) has written: "Psychoanalysts are satisfied that the integration of personality is more dependent on unconscious than on conscious coöperation. Something in the patient's mind desires 'wholeing' and sees to it that at the proper time the right material is brought forth in dreams and associations. We may call this personality the integrative design, the soul, or the higher self; the name does not matter. It matters that it exists, that it weaves strange patterns on the loom of dreams, gives us hints of depth within depth until, as a result of our educational efforts, a partnership develops between the patient's conscious and unconscious mind, serving the mysterious purposes of the latter without full comprehension on the part of the former."

This somewhat mystical statement expresses the truth that unconscious forces are constantly stretching up into experience and that these unconscious processes spin webs of association as they are expressed in dreams and fantasies.

However, there is no reason to believe that there is some innate or constitutional process which inevitably tends toward integration. Certainly it is not possible to posit some hypothetical autonomous force—the ego—for the ego is only the perceiving, thinking, and acting aspects of personality. On the contrary, there is reason to believe that integration is a function of growing intelligence and ability to conceptualize. As intelligence takes on stature, of necessity it tends to comprise more and more within its scope and it is only natural that as intelligence matures the child should begin to see relationships between the different elements of experience. It is always a feature of the higher mental processes to attempt to simplify its material. It seems certain that it is the concept of the self which enables the ego to fulfill its synthetic functions. To the extent that all aspects of personality are perceived in a clear, organized, and integrated fashion, then the ego is able to carry out its synthetic functions. It is the concept of the self which provides a possible consistency to behavior.

Gordon Allport (8), who has for many years upheld a theory of personality in terms of general traits, is of the belief that these general traits appear only under self-involvement. When the self is not involved, then behavior is of a specific nature, that is, there is no consistency or uniformity about it. A man might be truthful or helpful in one situation and not in another when he has not so much at stake. However, under pressure of self-involvement the ego takes on greater consistency and uniformity in its ways. Certain ideals of behavior are accepted and the ego takes pains to make its behavior live up to these ideals under diverse circumstances.

This tendency toward integration is also a function of the availability of different experiences to consciousness. Where large sectors of experience are repressed it is impossible for integration to achieve completeness. Integration depends upon self-regarding feelings. As self-esteem becomes greater the individual is able to reconcile different elements of his personality, whereas an individual with feelings of inferiority must hide from his own view those aspects of himself which he considers less lovely and acceptable and hence must destroy his own capacity for self-integration. One of the tasks of psychotherapy is to bring inaccessible parts of experience into consciousness where intelligence can assimilate them into the rest of the personality.

Integration depends on a time factor. The self is conceived as existing in a succession of units of time. The self is felt to be more consistent as it is recognized to be continuous and persistent over long periods of time. The most highly integrated persons are those who can review their lives over the total span and see themselves in the present as the flowering of earlier trends. This sense of continuity of the present with the past is necessary for ego integrity (45).

Ego integrity depends upon a certain stock of verbal symbols. The names and characterizations which one attaches to oneself help to achieve integration of personality and, by giving him a certain consistency of character, help him to unify his picture of himself.

Development of the Ego as a Social Phenomenon

Social psychologists stress integration as being a function of the structure of society. They insist that it is more difficult for individuals to be well integrated in a society which itself lacks integration and comprises within itself various forces and trends. Certainly the social aspect of integration must be fitted into the more individual aspects depending on intelligence and the ability to conceptualize.

In later development, group identification becomes increasingly a factor in ego formation. To the extent that society is cohesive and consistent it helps to form a strong and integrated ego. On the other hand, to the extent that society is stratified and specialized, it contains forces that are disruptive to the ego. When society lacks cohesiveness and consistency children are forced to base their egos on models that are shifting, sectional, and even contradictory.

One must recognize that the different culture groups, each with its different set of standards and expectations into which modern society is split up, represent hazards to ego integration. In particular, there is conflict between the expectations of an older and stabler society and the newer and more fluid society. Within our own society there are different goals, such as the coöperative versus the competitive, migratory versus sedentary trends, tendencies toward standardization as contrasted with individualization, tendencies toward uniformity in thinking versus independence and individuality in thinking. These various ego nuclei, which may be more pronounced in some individuals than in others, are fateful for the later strength and weakness of the ego. Where the individual is pulled in different directions he may find it difficult to adjust to new situations in which his previous tendencies are less appropriate.

Frustration and Ego Development

It has been said that while frustration and deprivation are necessary conditions for the establishment of the distinction between the self and other objects, they are not sufficient conditions for the establishment of this difference. Frustration initiates search but does not direct the search. Previous satisfactions and anticipation of future similar satisfactions direct the individual toward the object of his search. If wish coincides with reality there is a moment of illusion when a bit of experience (a baby taking the nipple) can be taken either as an inner experience or as external reality. So the infant learns to associate outer reality with his inner urges (205). There are three stages, then, in recognizing and accepting reality. In the first stage, there is an attempt to ignore the unpleasant as though it did not exist. The most primitive method of meeting a frustrating situation is to attempt a solution in fantasy or imagination and to pretend that the unpleasant situation does not exist. Fantasy itself has no brakes; fantasy can be brought under control only through the necessity of having to meet frustration imposed by reality. A second stage in accepting reality is to deny the unpleasant. This is a transition phase because the very act of denial at least admits its possibility to consciousness and shows that one is wavering between admitting it and ignoring it. The third stage is that of facing the unpleasant or mastering it either by withdrawal and giving up hope that it can yield pleasure or by attempting to modify the situation so that satisfaction can be achieved (62). The ego grows out of this conflict between fantasy and reality (66).

Experience teaches us that the satisfaction following a thoughtful solution when reality is recognized and accepted is more sure than the uncertainty of hallucinatory wishing. To imagine the bountiful meal may temporarily relieve distress, but increasingly the demands of real hunger destroy this illusory satisfaction. One may temporarily stave off the demand to stop and have lunch by recalling the many delicious meals that one has had in the past, but this kind of substitute satisfaction gradually loses its appeal. Eventually nothing will satisfy except real food. So we learn from experience that fantasy which ignores the unpleasant is a poor substitute for a real facing and mastering of the unpleasant situation.

Actually ambivalence is necessary for developing a sense of reality and integration (62). The same object which withholds satisfaction must be recognized as the source of satisfaction and hence it must be attended to. The mother whose absence is associated with the infant's hunger pangs is the same mother who later will bring food and relieve these hunger pangs. Therefore the absent mother cannot be ignored but must be attended to because she is the same mother who is the source of satisfaction. It is this "hate" of the mother for withholding satisfaction and "love" of the mother for providing satisfaction, then, that in a sense neutralize each other in the approach to reality. A baby has to learn that his primitive ruthlessness and impulse to destroy his mother because temporarily she withholds his pleasure defeats his purposes, and that he must learn to control his ruthless feelings because he needs this same mother to satisfy his needs. When the infant realizes that his mother, who hitherto has been undifferentiated from himself, cannot always be controlled, the realization helps him to differentiate himself from his mother.[1] The baby's missing and feeling after the breast may be thought of as a prototype of all later thought processes (62). The origin of the ego, then, and the development of a sense of reality are two aspects of this one developmental stage.

With too much frustration and too little satisfaction ego growth is retarded and reality is actually denied, for the pain is more than can be borne. In the face of too great deprivation of love the infant will turn to himself for satisfaction in the form of thumb-sucking or masturbation, and the child who is forced to love only himself prolongs his infancy. On the other hand, with too little frustration there is no stimulus to the differentiation of the self from the outside world, and hence there is no stimulus to ego growth. The development of the ego proceeds at a maximum pace, however, when there is more indulgence than deprivation, for indulgence helps to develop the sense of confidence and makes it possible for the infant to tolerate frustration and tension. The synthetic function of the ego helps to control ambivalence and to keep it functioning most adequately. Where the synthetic function of the ego is weak then ambivalence may get out of hand. It may, for instance, result in such splitting of the personality that the negative side may function without the regulation of the positive side. Where hate is not tempered by love, the integration of the personality is threatened. Or, if an individual finds it necessary to displace either hate or love onto another person, he may thereby manage his ambivalence but at the cost of personality integration. The best integrated individual is one who accepts reality and recognizes that the source of deprivation may also be the source of satisfaction.

---

[1] The language used to express a baby's feelings is inadequate. A baby's feelings are vague and undifferentiated as compared with adult feelings, even though they are violent and intense. But there is no terminology that does justice to infantile experience and it is necessary to approximate his feelings by using terms that are descriptive of adult behavior.

Identification in Ego Development

Identification is an important factor in the first stages of
ego development. The infant in his primitive attempts at
the mastery of stimuli tends to imitate what is perceived.
Mowrer (148), as a result of his observation of infants and of
birds that can approximate human speech, believes that the
first speech sounds are an attempt to substitute for the absent
parent. As Mowrer states it, when an infant's needs become
more intense and the parent is not there to fulfill them, the
infant may reproduce sounds that it has heard its mother
make as a method of substituting for her presence. In a similar
manner there may be a following with the eyes or a tracing
with the finger in an attempt to master and control situations,
and these primitive imitations may be the beginnings of perception.

Identifications help the ego to expand and broaden. Without a process of socialization an individual remains narrow,
provincial, and limited. Through identification he manages
to partake of the different forms of the culture around him
and to participate in it more fully.

One's identifications are an important factor in the integration of the ego. Through identification a child's drives are
given form in expression and thereby fused into a meaningful, purposeful pattern and hence are divested of specific elements of danger as might be the case were they to react impulsively and partially. Where father and mother present a
united and harmonious front to the child, he has a better
chance of growing up without warring factions within, but
where the child is pulled in his identifications in different
directions the result can be nothing more than conflict and
chaos within.

The need for identification becomes an incentive for a continuous learning process. Parents and teachers should recognize that the child's need for identification can be depended upon as one of the principal motives for learning.

Identification helps to determine the norms of masculinity or femininity in the growing child and will determine these important ingredients of personality in him as he matures. It is through these identifications that the child takes on his characteristic traits of dominance or submission, assertiveness or passivity, of attempting to control others or of acquiescing in the wishes and desires of others.

Development of Thinking

It is difficult to trace the beginnings of thought processes because their origins are shrouded in obscurity. The thinking processes of adults are studied largely through the help of language but before language is developed one has to depend upon observation and considerable speculation. There is no doubt that the language which is used in describing infantile modes of thinking is largely picturesque and inaccurate if the terms are to be used as they refer to similar adult phenomena. Infantile thinking is sometimes referred to in terms of omnipotence. Because the infant is so helpless and because he achieves his satisfactions through the assistance of other persons he depicts himself as a kind of Aladdin who only has to rub his lamp and the powerful genie comes to do his bidding (60). The infant finds that his cry will bring him succor, and helpless as he is, he feels all-powerful. As long as there is no clear concept of a separate object or person there is contentment in this feeling of unlimited power. Later, speech may substitute for the cry or for other gestures and signs by which the infant learns to control other people. This feeling of the magic power in the spoken word continues in many persons into later life and we have the use of incantation and prayer as a mode of meeting overwhelming need. It is only an easy transition to the belief in the omnipotence of ideas and there is a form of psychosis in which a person believes that he has extraordinary power through the influence of his ideas.

The development of the self destroys this infantile illusion of omnipotence. As the distinction between the self and other persons develops it becomes necessary for the infant to recognize his own weakness in comparison with the greater strength and skill of other persons. Growth of the self seems to require a clearer realization of the weakness and littleness of the self. Even as the ego increases in real strength and power as the child learns skills which enable him to master his surroundings, so there is at the same time a growth in familiarity with the weaknesses and limitations of the self (133).

Because this awareness of weakness in itself is threatening there is a tendency to project omnipotence onto others so that in a later stage of infancy the parents are looked upon as being all-powerful and all-wise individuals. This feeling of omnipotence in one's elders may continue on throughout childhood and may only be dispelled as a greater awareness of reality takes place later in adolescence. Some individuals, however, never outgrow their feeling of awe of and deference to the greater wisdom and power of their elders. This projection of omnipotence may extend beyond parent figures to rulers and to anyone who is in a position of authority. By believing in a supreme deity the individual bolsters himself in the light of his own feelings of weakness, helplessness, and inferiority.

In each of these projections there is also an identification. The little boy can add to his strength by feeling that *his* older brother or *his* father is a strong, important, and powerful man. One can add to his own feeling of strength by humbly asserting his belief in God.

MAGICAL THINKING

At the outset of thinking when acting and thinking are not fully differentiated there is resort to and belief in magic and magical processes. According to Piaget (159, p. 32) magical thinking takes place when an individual believes he can modify reality by wishing it. Magical thinking, then, is a substitution of pleasurable fantasy for unpleasant reality (59). Piaget (159) provides a number of fascinating illustrations. One child believed that if he counted up to a certain number between rattles in the radiator pipes in his room he would be saved from death. A boy believed he could influence the accuracy of his father's rifle shots by changing the angle of his father's cigar which he was holding. Another child believed that if he were to throw his favorite toy horse into the fire he would save his mother from death. These are examples of the fantasied relation between one's actions and other events. But as a second type one may fantasy a causal relation between one's *thoughts* and events. Tom Sawyer repeated a magic incantation to rid himself of a wart. A third type of magical thinking is to believe that there is some bond or connection between objects or places and events. A girl believed that there was a connection between the route she took to the dentist's office and being hurt by the dentist, and if he hurt her on any occasion she was careful to select a different route on her next visit. Finally magical thinking verges on animism as when a child does not use certain marbles because of a belief that they would have a tendency to return to their former owner. A clear illustration of magical thinking still remaining in our culture is the tendency to knock on wood when one has boasted that he has not been ill or has escaped accident for some time. This tendency may be interpreted by some as some sort of phylogenetic inheritance, but this explanation is farfetched and unnecessary. It does point

convincingly, however, to an infantile characteristic of thinking through which most individuals pass but out of which
many find it impossible to grow even under the encouragement of scientific knowledge.

The self and not-self are sometimes confused. What happens to another person or object might be experienced as
happening to the self, and, vice versa, what happens to the
self might be feared as possibly what might happen to someone else. The little child may interpret the death of some
relative or childhood playmate as portending some punishment or catastrophe that might happen to him, particularly
if he has felt hostile or jealous of the other person. On the
other hand, if the child is punished by being excluded from
the group he may interpret this as a threat of losing the close-
ness of his parents.

ANIMISM

Another feature of infantile thinking is the tendency to
invest objects in the world about one with feelings and
tendencies which pertain only to people or animals. This
primitive character of thinking which many persons never
wholly outgrow will invest objects with feeling as when one
says, "The key doesn't want to turn in the lock," or an animal with human characteristics as, "The bird is calling."
Actually the child in projecting his feelings onto objects is
thereby attempting to understand and master his inner bodily
processes and feelings.

Illustrations of animistic thinking in children are provided
by Piaget (159) as follows: One child says, "Every now and
then the moon disappears; perhaps it goes to see the man in
the clouds, or perhaps it's cold." Another says, "The bells
have waked up." A third child says, "When one walks, the
sun follows. When one turns around it turns around, too."

SYMBOLISM

Another feature of infantile thinking is the tendency toward symbolism. The object and the idea of the object are in some way confused and equated, or the object may be equated with some picture or model of the object, or the object and a part of the object in some way may be equated and confused. A photograph may serve as a token of a person who is absent or departed and may help to arouse the same feelings of affection, trust, or dependence which the person elicited in the flesh. In symbolism, similarities and identities are not distinguished and one may be satisfied with what looks like or feels like the real object of affection or fear. It is for this reason that children respond realistically to animals who may substitute for a person. A young child who wishes to sleep with his parents may be satisfied by being given as a substitute a toy animal or doll. A child may become frightened by a friendly dog who stands for his gruff and threatening father, or the child may be fascinated by the lion or tiger in the zoo because in some way it symbolizes the strength and fierceness which he admires and would like to have as his own attributes.

Symbolism may be of two types. In the simpler type one idea or object may substitute for another by virtue of crude and superficial similarity. This type of symbolism may take place before discrimination based on experience develops. It is at this early age that a hairy animal may symbolize the father because the child sees a similarity between the roughness and hairiness of the animal and the roughness and hairiness of his father. In later years when there is a greater capacity for discrimination these crude identities of infancy may seem crude and far-fetched, but psychoanalysts have demonstrated that they may be recalled again and again in dreams when critical faculties have been relaxed. A more complex type of symbolism is that in which a conscious idea may be used to substitute for and to hide an unconscious idea. This is the type of symbolism that is also found in dreams whereby some wish or feeling which is a repetition or counterpart of the previous day's experience is introduced into the dream as a substitute for and in order to hide some unacceptable and unconscious idea.

Symbolism marks a step forward in thinking. In the beginning the child does not differentiate between the symbol and that for which it stands. But as the symbol becomes detached from its object it can be manipulated mentally and can become a most potent intellectual tool. Language is just such a set of symbols that have become substituted for, or detached from, the objects for which they stand, and which are easily manipulated.

Another characteristic of infantile thinking is its use as a substitute for action, and psychoanalysts find that in later life many features of thinking may be reminiscent of some of the infant's activities. Thinking, for instance, may resemble tasting, looking, or touching in its exploratory nature. Learning has been likened to the taking in of food. Some people have a greediness whereby they wish to read scores of books and absorb everything that is known about a subject. Other forms of thinking may bear resemblances to excretory functions. Some loquacious individuals have been said to have a diarrhoea of words while others speak only with difficulty as though constipated. Thinking may also take on certain characteristics of sexual activities as, for instance, the curiosity which may bear similarity to sexual looking or touching. The boy who is inhibited from masturbation may find that mental activity can serve as a substitute. There are cases that have been reported in which mental activity and intellectuality have been overdeveloped as a substitute for a more emotional and sexual interest.

MATURE THINKING

It is not the place in this chapter to make a thorough analysis of the thinking process when it is fully developed, but merely to point out some of the origins of thinking. Thinking may also be considered an experimental living through or trying out of a course of action mentally before committing oneself to it in actuality (59). It is an anticipation in fantasy of what is probable. Thinking originally is for the purpose of social adaptation and only later can it be divorced from its original function and become a pleasurable or defensive activity in itself. The intellect, then, is the ego's tool for solving problems.

Psychologists have thought of intelligence as being primarily a function of innate neural structure and organization. However, recent clinical data would indicate that the intellect is also a function of developmental experience. Intelligence, for instance, depends upon a high evaluation of the self and an adequate ego. The person who has to struggle with attitudes about himself is hindered from giving his attention to external problems. To maximize a child's functioning intellect, his self-evaluation must be maximized—he must believe in himself and in his capacities.

Logical thinking presupposes a strong ego, and is as much a matter of character as of intellect (59). Effective thinking involves the capacity to postpone action. In order to think effectively one must be able to tolerate tensions. It is usually found that the strong thinker is also the individual who is rich in countercathexes, that is, in interests which run counter to his natural impulses and keep them in check. It takes courage and mental freedom to notice something not generally accepted. To be able to think effectively one must also be able to distinguish between a painful past and a hopeful future. One must be able to endure recalling the disappointments of the past as well as to look ahead to the future without the dread which memories of the past lead one to expect.

The strong thinker is ready to judge reality on the basis of experience with a minimum of interference from his needs and desires. Logical thinking implies the faculty of considering phenomena objectively rather than in relation to the self. The individual who finds that he is personally involved in an issue which is being discussed in a group will not be able to consider the issue freely and objectively. His own involvement prevents him from full freedom in considering all of the factors. The individual who is personally involved is unable to consider the needs of other persons on a par with his own. It is for this reason that it is difficult for members of a family to think objectively with regard to family problems and issues. Each family member has his own interests at stake in any issue that may come up and this makes it difficult for him to consider the interests of the family as a whole, apart from his own individual needs. Effective thinking can take place only when confidence and security have been developed and are present.

Independence is one criterion of maturity. It is characteristic of the dependent child to look to his parents for assistance in working out problems. When he goes to school he expects assistance from his teachers and reluctantly takes responsibility for the accuracy of his own work. He must continually look to others for verification. It is a mark of maturity to be able to tackle a problem independently, to try out the various possibilities without assistance, and to have one's own inner criteria of success. But the good thinker never wholly cuts himself off from communication with others; rather he draws suggestions and ideas from every possible source.

Although thinking helps an individual to adjust to reality,

it may also take on other functions. Thinking may serve as a defense in the individual's attempt to avoid his painful and dangerous impulses. The ego can use thinking as a sublimation in adjustment to reality. Blos (23) describes an adolescent boy, Paul, who is struggling with the conflict to remain a child and to retain his position with his mother, on the one hand, and to grow up and become more mature in his relations with his peers, on the other. He puts aside, however, facing this dilemma directly, and attempts to work it out through his interests in mathematics and language and his endless debates on philosophical and religious issues. Overstressing the intellectual helps the individual adopt an ascetic attitude and at the same time carries with it a high amount of social prestige.

Rôle of Language in the Development of the Ego

Notwithstanding the importance of language in aiding in the integration of the ego, it is apparent that the ego begins to take form long before language appears. To be sure, thinking before language is extremely rudimentary. The ego that develops before language must be based on kinesthetic, visual, and auditory cues and the symbolic nature of the reactions must be of an extremely rudimentary form. However, it is believed that every single thought, even in the adult, before it is formulated in words, has come through a prior wordless state. Before the thought receives its verbal formulation it is present in inner tensions which indicate the need expressed and the direction of the activity which is indicated. Nevertheless, acquisition of speech and the rational use of speech become decisive steps in the formation of the ego (59). After the first year, when speech normally becomes effective, the growth of the ego accelerates. Speech helps to anticipate events more precisely, effectively and realistically. There are many who believe that the ego achieves its consolidation only after there is thinking on a conceptual basis, that is, symbolic and verbal.

Survey of the Stages of Ego Development

During the first year, the infant makes a beginning at establishing independence from his mother. He begins to perceive the mother as a separate person and likewise makes a beginning of sensing himself as a person. In his helplessness the infant has to rely upon such devices as crying to command the attention and services of others. Consequently this is spoken of as the stage of omnipotence when the infant because of his helplessness feels all-powerful. At ages two and three there is a beginning of real ego competence as the toddler begins to run about and manipulate objects and people for his own purposes. This is the stage when with the growing realization of his own powers and the beginnings of self-sufficiency the child may become obstinate and resistant. Recognizing his own helplessness he projects his fantasies of greatness onto his parents. At this stage the child comprehends only the external shape and appearance of phenomena without being able to explain them rationally. His thinking operates by making comparisons and by seeing the analogies and likenesses and differences between phenomena.

Not until the age of four or five does the child's thinking mature so as to take on the form resembling that which it will have as an adult. At this stage the child becomes interested in personal relationships. He becomes aware of the relationships between his parents, is curious about them, and reacts to them as his own interests dictate. He wants to understand these relationships and his own relationship to others. It is at this stage that the first conceptions of causality and logic begin to appear (133). Now the child is able to consider phenomena somewhat objectively without referring them at all times to his own needs and desires. Negativism is replaced by growing social adaptability. However, few individuals become wholly independent of parental support or authority in their thinking by integrating the scientific point of view into all of life's compartments. It is significant that even the most distinguished scientists who have long ago cast aside dependence on others in their bold exploration into unknown territory in the area of their special competence may still cling to presumptions which they docilely accept in the more homely aspects of living in which they are not "expert."

If the emotional problems at the age of four and five have been successfully worked through, the normal child then passes into a stage—known as the latency period—in which a certain stability is achieved. Because he has temporarily and to an extent resolved his emotional problems, the normal child during the years from six to twelve can devote his attention to learning about the world around him and to perfecting motor and social skills and establishing self-control. The child who has not successfully worked through the earlier emotional problems will continue to struggle with these throughout this period of middle childhood.

Adolescence, however, tends to disrupt this equilibrium, at least in our culture. As new drives come into prominence the ego is confronted with new tasks of adjustment and integration. First of all, the ego has to adjust itself to physical changes in this last stage of growth. The ego must become familiar with these new physical phenomena and learn to accommodate itself to them. Since the body is representative of the self the adolescent boy or girl feels doubts and confusions about the self and is either plunged into overconfidence or into feelings of inadequacy.

In adolescence there is a repetition of the infantile struggle with the basic drives of love and hate. At times these drives appear to get out of hand and there is a continuous effort to master them and to bend them toward the demands of adult living. The ego is afraid of and hostile to these drives because they represent a recrudescence of the earlier œdipal struggles. Erotic demands become increasingly powerful and if the adolescent was confronted with guilts and doubts over these same erotic impulses in infancy, they may trouble him in adolescence. With some adolescents these drives may get out of hand but in other cases they may be strongly repressed. Likewise the adolescent ego fears aggressive and hostile impulses, particularly if there are remnants of the conflict and guilt over them coming down from the œdipal conflict. Like the erotic impulses, these aggressive drives may also break over and become unruly during adolescence or they may be severely repressed. The adolescent may doubt his right to and ability to love or his worthiness to be loved. Likewise he may have doubts about his manliness and vigor or about his ability to stand up to those who challenge his stamina.

The ego may be strong or weak during adolescence according to the strength it inherits from its infantile experiences. Intellectual interests may help the adolescent boy or girl to master the excitement from the new driving forces at this period.

Flightiness is a well-known characteristic of adolescence which again represents the ebb and flow of the struggle of the ego to gain the upper hand over surging forces within (77). Stability in adolescence may be helped or hindered by the aid given by adults. If the adolescent is associated with tolerant and accepting adults who at the same time give their firm coöperation in helping him control his impulses, ego development may proceed normally. If, on the other hand, adults are unnecessarily repressive, demanding, critical, or punitive, the adolescent boy or girl may be forced to side with his impulses in combating these adults who are his enemies. Or if the adults are lax and easy-going the adolescent is at the mercy of his own inner impulses, since he receives no outer assistance in keeping them under control. This striving for adult stability is not accomplished easily and the struggle may persist over several years.

Although mental capacity reaches its maximum development in the early twenties, this does not at all mean that the actual functions of the ego and the capacity to adjust need stop developing and expanding all through life. At all stages of adulthood an individual has the capacity to learn more adequate reality testing, better integration, more effective control and direction of his energies. There are few, if any, totally integrated individuals who have succeeded in developing a wholly harmonious personality whose reality testing enables them to think objectively and rationally and whose self-esteem enables them to act according to their own needs as well as the needs of others. The fact of the matter is that most individuals do not thus continue with the development of the ego. Apparently one enlarges and expands his ego functions only under the stress of circumstances, and most persons who settle themselves down to comfortable living make no effort to continue the development of their adaptive capacities. When the ego no longer practices the task of adapting itself to new circumstances common observation leads to the conclusion that it tends to lose the capacity to make such adaptations.

5

DEVELOPMENT OF THE SELF

Like the ego, the self as a percept is not present at birth but begins to develop gradually as perceptive powers develop. Charles Darwin (42) in a resumé of a diary account which he kept of the infancy of one of his children observed that at four and a half months the infant responded to a mirror reflection of himself as a real object in the outside world, but that two months later he understood that it was an image of himself. Probably this child was somewhat precocious. Children may stand before a mirror and babble in a social way long before they give evidence of recognizing the image as their own.

The self develops as we feel ourselves separate and distinct from others, but the first differentiations are dim and hazy. It is probably true that one learns to recognize and distinguish others before one learns to recognize and distinguish the self. Normally at about eight months an infant begins to differentiate faces, and at this time shyness may develop which probably signifies that the infant differentiates between a familiar and an unfamiliar face. As the recognition of the familiar face takes shape, vague notions of the self simultaneously develop. As the mother begins to take shape as a separate person the baby forms vague notions of himself as a separate individual.

A baby learns to differentiate himself from others as he

interacts with them—as he is handled, fondled, played with, fed, or bathed by his mother. A baby who is neglected has difficulty in forming a clear perception of himself. A child can only learn to know himself in terms of the treatment he receives from others around him.

Perception is an important factor in this process of differentiation. When the source of satisfaction is temporarily withdrawn the infant is forced to perceive in order to find the source of satisfaction. A vague realization develops that something has to be done by the outside world and this leads to the first longing and directing of attention toward outer objects. Benedek (17), as a result of her observations, believes that the infant's first perception is the recognition of the face of the mother, coming even before the recognition of objects such as the bottle.

The infant's realization that the mother (hitherto undifferentiated from self) cannot always be controlled helps to produce that differentiation. This sorting and interpreting of stimuli helps to make the infant respond to himself as being apart and different from the world around him. The outer world is recognized in its independence of the self by the process of search and comparison. First the baby makes signs of his anticipation and of his expectation of the coming of his mother and this is followed by his recognition of her footsteps, of her singing, of the sounds that she makes in preparing his food, and then finally of her presence itself. There is not only a need to perceive this but to recognize a distinction between one's own action and the action of others. There is a growing realization of his dependence on persons and things outside himself and of his efforts to adjust himself to them. Growing awareness of this distinction between himself and others may be marked by his fierce opposition to the wishes of others in the second year. But recognition of the differences between the self and others must be paralleled by a recognition of the similarities between the self and others.

At the beginning the self is recognized as a self-assertive feeling (40). The first sensations of the self come through the kinesthetic sensations, and it is only later that awareness of and reference to the body makes self-consciousness a more vivid experience.

Rôle of the Body Image in the Development of the Self

Some writers, particularly Schilder (178), have emphasized the importance of the body image in the development of the self and have asserted that the child's perception of its own body becomes the nucleus of awareness of the self. Hoffer (112) believes that in early infancy the hands and the mouth convey the first sensations of the self. Horowitz (115) asked children and adults to tell where the self was located or "where you are." The adults most often located the self in the head, mentioning specifically the brain, eyes and face; less often then mentioned heart, hands and genitals. Children tended to localize the self in various parts of the body. However, Horowitz believes that this sort of an inquiry has little significance: localization of the self in a part of the body may have some significance as a reference point, but actually he believes the localization is superficial and has little reality.

As the perception of the body becomes more and more distinct, feelings relative to the body also become more and more clearly differentiated, but feelings, like perception, emerge only gradually, apparently first in the so-called "erogeneous zones"—lips, arms, nipples, genital organs, ear lobe, tongue, palms of the hands, and forehead—and later in other areas of the body equipped with sensory nerve endings. But as Federn (52) points out, each of these new acquisitions becomes a fixation point and in neurotic or psychotic regression there may be a return to these fixation points.

It is important in this regard to differentiate between the inner and outer body. The external body, that is, the body that can be seen and felt to the touch is easier to learn about and is actually discovered earlier than the inner body. A little child can only imagine what the interior of the body is like and he pictures it in terms of models of machines or containers with which he is familiar in the everyday world (179). Knowledge of the interior of the body remains a mystery for most persons throughout life, for actually a true understanding of what lies beneath the skin becomes the property only of surgeons or students of anatomy and physiology.

The external body becomes differentiated from the rest of the world by the simultaneous occurrence of both outer tactile sensation and inner sensory data. We learn about ourselves when by pressing a finger on a spot on the skin we receive sensations from the skin. The body then becomes learned by the coördination of what can be seen and what can be felt. Actually when the finger touches the skin there are two simultaneous sensory touch impressions. One is the impression of the touching finger and the other is the impression of the part of the body which is touched. The self becomes differentiated from other selves largely because of the difference in tactile sensation. Pinching another person results in no feeling of pain whereas pinching oneself results in pain. The recognition of the body grows out of these pleasurable and painful experiences. Actually we learn to know our bodies better from pain than from pleasure because pain sensory endings are spread over the total surface of the body whereas sensations of pleasure are concentrated in a few erotic zones.

It should be recognized that the body image does not coincide with the objective body but is distorted (178). A good illustration of this may be found in listening to one's own voice in a mechanical recording. Experience is fairly widespread that an individual does not recognize his own voice when he hears it being played back to him from the recording. This only means that the impression which he has built up concerning his voice does not correspond to the impression that he gets when he hears his voice coming to him from a distance. The bodily self that we feel does not necessarily correspond to the bodily self which others may observe.

The body occupies a middle position between the external world and the self as the agent of our perceiving, thinking and acting (19). Our hair can be cut off or a tooth may fall out and become detached from our body. The body can be viewed more externally and objectively than our inner tensions, thoughts, and feelings. The sense of the self proceeds largely from increasing differentiation and localization of body experiences. As the little child learns to identify and point to his nose, mouth, eyes, and ears, he is beginning to form a more detailed picture of himself. But the image that we form of these facial features comes not so much from the tactual sensations of feeling, but the visual sensation of seeing those same features in others. A baby learns what his ear is like by noting what his father's or his mother's ear looks like. In many ways our conceptions of ourselves are reflections of what we perceive others to be. Later there is a further differentiation of the self as a body and the self as a mind which can experience sensations and feelings, solve problems, and make decisions. Throughout this development, however, the body remains as a very solid and substantial core to which the less tangible experiences of the self can be referred.

With regard to concepts of the inside of the body and their coördination with inner feelings, psychologists have pointed out that the little child tends to associate his inner states with outer objects and persons. In particular, the inner states of tension and need are associated with the withholding and bad parent. On the other hand, inner states of satisfaction and contentment are associated with the providing, attentive, and good parent. Consequently we conceive of inner states of tension and need as bad and think of ourselves as bad when distressing inner states are present, because we associate them with the bad withholding parent. We also think of ourselves as good when in a state of contentment and satisfaction, because then we associate ourselves with the good and providing parent.

Of special importance is the discovery of differences between the sexes, facts which every boy and girl must eventually learn. These differences come inevitably as a shock when first discovered, perhaps more so to a girl than to a boy. Later in adolescence there is the need to adjust to still further signs of sex difference, and the ability to accept these signs and to fit easily into the rôle that society defines for the two sexes contributes considerably to the stability of adolescent adjustment.

The body is particularly valued and becomes the core of later self value because it is the source of pleasure and pain and because it is the tool or the vehicle for achieving satisfaction. Not only does satisfaction take place within the body but also the body, after skills of grasping, locomotion, and control of the eyes have been acquired, becomes a tool for attaining satisfaction.

Extensions of the Self

In later development extensions of the body become important, and anything that extends the effectiveness or control which is originally a bodily function then can be called one's own. Clothes become closely identified with the body and in fact determine the shape and character of the body which we present to the outside world. In this way, toys, tools, and possessions serve as extensions of the body and help to widen the sense of self. Later on our position and our wealth become further extensions of the body. A boy's pockets will contain valued possessions which enhance his prestige and give him a sense of greater power and control. Even our ideals and social values can be thought of as extensions of what were originally bodily functions. Inasmuch as we value our bodies and do what is necessary to preserve and protect them, the body image becomes the basis of sympathy and we learn to value the bodies and possessions of others as we have learned to value our own.

Eventually the self indicates all the meanings and evaluations that a person has about himself and his relations to the world around him. An individual absorbs into and as part of himself all of the persons, objects, ideas, and ideals with which he identifies himself.

Plaint of Complexity

I have too many selves to know the one.
In too complex a schooling was I bred,
Child of too many cities, who have gone
Down all bright cross-roads of the world's desires,
And at too many altars bowed my head
To light too many fires.

One polished self I have, she who can sit
Familiarly at tea with the marquise
And play the exquisite
In silken rustle lined with etiquette,
Chatting in French, Italian, what you please,
Of this and that—

*   *   *   *   *   *

And I've a modern, rather mannish self,
Lives gladly in Chicago.
She believes
That woman should come down from off her shelf
Of calm dependence on the male
And labor for her living.

She likes men,
And equal comradeship, and giving
As much as she receives.

* * * * * *

I've a self compound of strange, wild things—
Of solitude, and mud, and savagery;
Loves mountain-tops, and deserts,
And the wings
Of great hawks beating black against the sky.

* * * * * *

I've a self might almost be a nun,
So she loves peace, prim gardens in the sun
Where shadows sift at evening,
Hands at rest,
And the clear lack of questions in her breast.

* * * * * *

And deeper yet there is my mother self,
Something not so much I as womankind,
That surges upward from a blind
Immeasurable past.

* * * * * *

The best I am, or can be
This self stands
When others come and go, and in her hands
Are balm for wounds and quiet for distrations,
And she's the deepest source of all my actions.

* * * * * *

But I've another self she does not touch,
A self I live in much, and overmuch
These latter years.
A self who stands apart from outward things,
From pleasure and from tears,
And all the little things I say and do.
She feels that action traps her, and she swings
Sheer out of life sometimes, and loses sense
Of boundaries and of impotence.

* * * * * *

> But what she sees in her far spirit world,
> Or what the center is
> Of all this whirl of crowding I's,
> I cannot tell you—only this
> That I've too many selves to know the one.
>   —EUNICE TIETJENS [1]

The self is the most real thing in our experience, and is the frame of reference with which a person perceives, conceives, and evaluates the world around him and toward which he reacts.

It should be evident from this discussion that the self has a periphery as well as a core. The core Snygg and Combs (192, p. 112) have called the self-concept, which they define as "these parts of the phenomenal field which the individual has differentiated as definite and fairly stable characteristics of himself." It is probable that the stability which these authors believe to determine the core of the self may be found to depend on those early experiences in infancy out of which the first glimpses of the self develop. To call a person a liar somehow strikes at something which threatens his sense of personal integrity, while to comment on his poor pronunciation of French may hardly cause a ripple.

Rôle of Language in the Development of the Self

Language also helps to clarify the concept of the self. The use of the proper name helps a child identify himself and accelerates the development of self awareness (191). Those who have studied the development of children's use of self-reference words tell us that a child uses the names of others before he uses his own name. Traditionally a child's first words are "mama" and "papa," which at first may be nothing more than natural mouthing coupled with the emittance of sound.

[1] Taken from M. W. Calkins, *The Persistent Problems of Philosophy* (New York: The Macmillan Company, 1907, 1917, 1925).

We are also told that a child uses his proper name before he uses the pronouns "mine," "me," and "I." This is understandable as a child is referred to by others by his Christian name and the pronouns he learns only by inference as individuals refer to themselves. In general children are using the personal pronouns by the third year. According to a study by Fisher (63), no child used "me," "our," or "us" until the first half of the third year. Another observation reported is that children tend to use the first person singular more frequently in playing with other children than they do in their conversation with adults (97). Apparently children are stimulated to assert themselves more directly with others of their own age. Singular and plural pronouns in the third person are used more frequently with adults in these early stages.

Awareness of Self

Philosophers have been intrigued by the distinction between consciousness and self-consciousness. Consciousness refers to the general vividness and sensitiveness of our experiences when we are awake and give our attention to what goes on about us. Self-consciousness is a partial aspect of the whole realm of consciousness when attention is given to the self. Self-consciousness involves a backward look. When an act is performed it may be conscious but not self-conscious. Self-consciousness comes after the act as one turns back to look at it, to recall and to think about it. It is even possible to take a third step and to look back at our own self-awareness so that one can be conscious of his own self-consciousness. In general, the looking back and recalling of an experience seems to have a peculiar degree and intensity of conscious awareness which differs from that which adheres to the original experience. Self-consciousness comes around the age of two, although it has its vaguer beginnings before this time.

Self as Perceived and Self as Conceived

We perhaps should make a distinction between the self as perceived and the self as conceived. Certainly the self as perceived comes earlier. A baby begins to explore parts of his body with his eyes and his hands and learns to identify them by name and by touch. To be able to integrate these separate sense impressions into a concept of the self as a separate entity comes later. Snygg and Combs (192, p. 94) express this same point of view when they state that "this ability to see oneself from the point of view of another develops somewhat later in the individual than his phenomenological self." The "I" concept develops only as maturity and the advent of language make conceptualization possible. The concept of the self comes after the recognition and conceptualization of others (13). As Mead (145) has emphasized, we tend to respond to ourselves as others have responded to us. As a matter of fact our concept of ourselves is built up very largely from the reactions and attitudes toward us expressed by others. As a child is labelled pretty, bright, stubborn, awkward, cute, he tends to live up to this concept that others help him to form of himself. A child develops self-feeling also in part by taking on the rôle of other persons. As a child identifies himself with his parents and his brothers and sisters and attempts to copy them in his methods of eating, dressing, playing with toys, and the like, he develops more definite feelings of himself. However, there are occasions when the concept of the self departs from the practice of those about, when the culture changes but the person is still responding to old ideas of himself. The boy or girl going to college may continue to think of himself as he grew up in his home town and as he was thought of by parents and neighbors, and may find it difficult to accept the patterns of conduct and thinking exhibited all around him in his new environment.

Self Identity

In this connection the concept of *self identity* is helpful. Every individual, to a certain extent, identifies himself as a unique individual. This depends in part on his recognition through memory of his own continuity in time and, in part, on the fact that other persons recognize him today as the same individual he was yesterday. Self identity involves in addition a synthesis of these two forms of recognition. The inner feeling of continuity and sameness (I am the same person that took a new job a year ago, married five years ago, graduated from college ten years ago, played with the gang twenty years ago) must somehow be linked up with the feeling that others recognize me as the same person, too ("I can remember you when you were a little boy—my, how you've grown!"). When one is recognized by a friend on the street or when one's enduring position in society is recognized and admitted, he is helped to maintain his self identity. Individuals resist change. To lose one's self identity is a threat to the permanence of the self and such a threat is likely to topple other values along with it. Also, when there is a break in the continuity of memories as in aphasia we have states of dissociation, fugue states, split personalities.

Snygg and Combs (192, p. 85) attempt to explain inconsistencies in behavior, as when a man is churlish to his employees but obsequious to his superior officers, in terms of the vagaries of the concept of the self. This explanation, true as far as it goes, is only half an explanation, omitting as it does the unconscious factors in attitude and the origin of attitudes in previous experience. A man may have learned in the past to be respectful to father figures but domineering over younger siblings.

Although the development of the concept of the self marks a step forward in development, at the same time it may temporarily interfere with adjustment. As the baby shifts his attention from the mastery of the world about him to attention to himself he may become for a brief time more self-centered and hence more difficult in his social relations. Indeed, it is well known that the younger the child the more egocentric he is, the development of social feeling being a somewhat later development. The beginning of self-awareness may also arouse self-consciousness and embarrassment. A little child of two may suddenly become shy of those whom he knows slightly but who are not members of his family. This shyness probably indicates a step forward in self-awareness. It is during the second year that negativism and resistance develop and undoubtedly this is in some way due to the growing awareness of the self as a separate entity with independence from others. As one writer puts it "obstinacy and rebellion are useful in toughening the ego (self)." But too much attention to the self will interfere with adjustment to the world at all stages. Frequently the child who is prevented from feeling secure to explore about him is thrown back to give undue attention to himself and his body to the detriment of his adjustment to the world about.

The Self as Conceived and the Self to be Realized

Another distinction may be made between the self as conceived and the self to be realized. At a somewhat later stage concepts of the possibilities of the self begin to develop as parents and teachers point out the direction of possible growth and emphasize goals to be striven for, and an ego-ideal (which according to our terminology should be called a "self-ideal") begins to take form. A child adopts ideals to be achieved in the future for the simple reason that in the present he is weak and helpless. The more weak and helpless, the more grandiose the ideal. The self-ideal takes shape to help the weak child to adapt to the stronger reality which he sees around him.

And one way in which wounded self-respect can be healed is to gratify narcissistic needs by creating and introjecting an ideal self in fantasy. Later in the discussion of level of aspiration (see pp. 90 ff.) we shall see that the self as conceived and the self to be realized are not identical, that they may conflict with one another, and that one may play upon and influence the other.

Development of the Self as a Social Phenomenon

Writers on social psychology have stressed the social determinants of the self, and this is the theme of the book on *The Psychology of Ego Involvements* by Sherif and Cantril (191). According to Snygg and Combs (192, p. 86), the self is formed only as the individual defines his relation to the world about him. "The culture in which we move is so completely and inextricably a part of our experience as to overshadow almost all else in determining the nature of the phenomenal self developed by each of its members. Even our definitions and values with respect to the purely physical aspects of our environment are not left entirely to our own experience but are colored, interpreted, and valued one way or another by the culture into which we are born, as they are interpreted to us by the acts of the people who surround us." Snygg and Combs, in elaborating their phenomenological point of view, indicate that all meaningful perceptions derive their meaning from the self already in existence. In other words, we tend to interpret all experiences in terms of what they mean to us personally. The specific form which the self will take varies according to the relation of the child with adults, with the opportunities which the social environment provides, with the opportunities for language development, with contact with cultural products and symbols, and with the give-and-take association with age contemporaries. Gesell finds that a child will set standards for himself typically by 72 months (6 years). A child's attitude toward himself will be realistic if others take a reasoned and sensible attitude toward him, but his concept of himself will be distorted to the extent that others express unfair attitudes about him.

The concept of group consciousness and of group identification is necessary for the further development of the self. A child has to learn that he is a boy and different from a girl, that he is white and different from a Negro, that he is poor and different from those that are rich. In these perceptions of difference the child is learning to identify himself with a group or groups and these group identifications are intrinsic aspects of the development of the self (116).

For this reason membership in a group and awareness of this membership is an integral part of the formation of the self. Individuals who live in extreme isolation fail to form adequate percepts and concepts of the self. As Hilgard (111) has said, "the self, as a social product, has full meaning only when expressed in social interaction." Snygg and Combs (192, p. 138) point out that not only does the self develop by perceiving group differences but also by being sensitive to group expectations. Society expects different reactions from boys and girls, from the young and old, from the rich and poor, from the educated and uneducated, from members of different occupations.

Development of the self is necessary before it is possible for a child to be competitive, coöperative, sympathetic, or before he can set goals and levels of aspiration. Some self-development must take place before such trends as race prejudice, political bias, or religious affiliation can appear (190).

Shifts in attitude toward a person by others are reflected by changes in the attitude of the person toward himself. When one is with others who admire him he feels confident, but when he moves over to a group that is critical then his self-confidence wanes. The developing self becomes less stable and less secure in the midst of changing and inconsistent situations.

In spite of the fact that the perception of the self reflects the way in which the individual is perceived by others and their expressions of attitude toward him, there is still considerable disparity between the perception of oneself and others' perception of him. A person is frequently astonished to be told how he hesitates when he speaks, or how he monopolizes the conversation, or how he walks with his head down, gaze concentrated on the sidewalk before him. We may give the world the impression of our self-confidence and security and no one may know how we shake in our shoes. We may impress the world as being gay and carefree while we are weighted down with care and worries.

Development of Self in Adolescence and Old Age

During later adolescence, the individual is struggling to work out a new concept of the self which leaves behind the dependence of childhood and attains the independence and self-direction of maturity. New self ideals which may persist throughout life are taken on during adolescence, for this is the period when ideals are adopted. Havighurst (109), who has supplied some new data on the formation of ideals, points out that children first select their parents as their ideals; then in later childhood and early adolescence they pick out romantic and glamorous figures to admire—the airplane pilot or the movie star. Only with developing maturity will admiration for more intrinsic qualities of character begin to appear. But at all stages the ideal self is influenced by a child's surroundings. Havighurst believes his evidence points to a fact that many have noted from common observation—that ideals are formed more from identification with parents, teachers, clergy, and age contemporaries than from what one reads or is taught. The ideal self comes from accepting the characteristics of people of prestige and honor in the community. Status values are increasingly derived from age contemporaries in adolescence in contrast to the ideals which stemmed from parents in earlier childhood. Self values also are subject to modification during the adolescent period. At the beginning of adolescence, as threats to the older established self-values begin to appear, in consequence of doubts concerning his ability to meet expectations of himself and of others, there is an increased selfishness and he becomes more self-centered. The ability of a boy or a girl to take on more altruistic interests and to participate in group activities is a sign that adolescent development is proceeding normally.

In old age the ego must make still another adjustment. As one's powers begin to wane and one's importance to others diminishes there arises a distinct threat to the self. It requires a special strength of character to give up responsibilities of middle life and to gracefully accept the facts of aging with the inevitable debasement of the self. Individuals with resources for continued activity and production are best able to maintain their self-respect as their powers diminish.

6

SELF-FEELING AND SELF-VALUATION

Self-Feeling

It is necessary to make a distinction between self-awareness and self-feeling, for feeling may accompany consciousness with varying degrees of strength (54). It is possible to have aware- ⌣ ness of the self without accompanying feelings.[1] On the other hand, it is not possible to have feeling about the self without awareness. Normally the self is reacted to with a variety of such feelings as elation, depression, contentment, irritation, and the like. Just as one can be aware of the presence of other people and yet have very little feeling for them, so it is possible to be aware of the self and yet react to the self with little or no feeling. A young lady who was disappointed in love remarked on looking at a photograph of herself and her beau that she had no feeling about him or herself in the picture. It was as though she was looking at a picture of two other persons whom she did not know.

We are told that the nucleus of self-feeling comes from the sensations of equilibrium and space, that is, those senses which arise from the semicircular canals in the middle ear (54, 59). Our feelings about ourselves come first of all from our orientation in space as we feel ourselves seated in a certain room,

---

[1] There are some who believe that every perception is accompanied by feelings of greater or less intensity, but it is also possible that the feelings which normally accompany perception may be repressed.

striding along over a certain road, or hurtling through space in a plane.

It is possible to separate feelings for the body from feelings for the mental processes, but this distinction is never too sharp. Normally self-feeling extends to the whole body, but in regression the feeling for certain parts of the body, particularly the extremities, may be lost first and feelings with regard to face and head normally are the last to be lost. Also the bodily self normally disappears before the mental self. We can observe this in falling asleep, also in fainting—the body is the first to slide away and down, and the last to disappear is the awareness of our own thought. There may be a similar partial dissociation of the self from the body in states of reverie while awake. This comes out particularly clearly in dreams, for in dreams there is no feeling for the body but everything is in terms of reactions, relations, and the give and take between people (54). In a dream one's feelings for one's self as a person in a body seem not to be present.

Self-feelings may be either active or passive. On the one hand, one may have a feeling or attitude of self-assertion, of confidence, of being in control of the situation, of directing oneself forward in a purposeful activity. On the other hand, one may have the feeling of being the victim of circumstances, of being helpless and dependent, and of having things happen to one's self over which one does not have much control. Normal living is a combination of these dual feelings of self-direction and helplessness.

Self-feeling plays an essential part in the uninterrupted or restored unity of the self. A normal person feels himself to have a continuity over a period of time as was stated on page 73. It is also normal for a person to feel an essential unity between his mental processes and his body. He feels that he has certain control of himself and that he is to a degree responsible for his actions and a master of his own destiny. The absence of these feelings is found in some of the well-known pathological mental conditions.

A certain degree of self-feeling is essential for normality. It is normal and healthy for an individual to experience the self with a certain degree of warmth, familiarity, and intimacy. Such healthy self-feeling is the basis for happiness (53). Without such self-feeling the individual feels heavy, dead, lifeless, and life holds no meaning or zest. With mere knowledge of the self, without feeling, the self is experienced as something insufficient and incomplete, an experience almost akin to fear.

In certain pathological states there may be a diminution of self-feeling when there is an exclusion of physical and mental activities as well as of the body from self-awareness, so that what one does and what one thinks seems to be foreign to the self. Such states represent a partial destruction of the self. For instance, fatigue sometimes brings on a kind of depression in which one becomes only dimly aware of the body and its processes. Some writers have referred to this depersonalization as a kind of oceanic feeling and they recognize it as a regression to the mental state of infancy before clear awareness of the self has taken place (125). Some neurotic individuals have similar minor disturbances of self feeling. Some individuals, for instance, have difficulty reëstablishing themselves in the morning, and it takes some time before they "feel like themselves" and are able to take active part in the affairs of the day (54).

This depersonalization is recognized in some cases to be a defense mechanism, a method that the ego adopts to hide from itself its feelings of inadequacy and inability to cope with problems that may arise. With feelings of the self deadened the ego does not have to confront some of the threats from its own failures.

Self-Valuation—Self-Esteem

SELF AS A CENTRAL OR ORGANIZING VALUE

No sooner does the self begin to take form in early childhood than values begin to accrue to it and it is not long before the self becomes the principal value around which life revolves (149). Self-love finds its origin at the start of life as an infant finds pleasure in the stimulation of certain sensitive bodily zones. A baby's first love is eating, for it is in the act of nursing and in the stimulation of lips, gums, and tongue, that the little baby first finds pleasure. At first this pleasure is entirely receptive, but later on the infant becomes more energetic and this pleasure enters a more active stage. There is a wish to swallow, to control, to dominate others, and an attempt to win satisfaction by active effort.

Love also finds expression in connection with the processes of excretion. The term *anal eroticism* is used to indicate the expression of love through the excretory processes. In early infancy anal erotic love expresses itself by the wish to give, to expel, to reject, throw away, lose, or destroy the object (urine or feces). In a later stage when toilet habits have been established, anal erotic love turns to a wish to retain, to master, and control the object. This is the basis for expressions of love in the form of hoarding and saving and also for those forms of self-love which show themselves in self-willed independence.

The little child shows self-love through fondness for the body and its products. For instance, there is an early desire to exhibit the body and to display it to others who are interested. This perhaps arises from the mother's intense interest in the child's body. A little child desires to continue the early admiration which parents showed toward him by continued display of the body. Later, of course, these tendencies are repressed, and the child tends to inhibit exhibitionistic tendencies, but many older children, in spite of the general expectation, are fond of displaying their naked bodies, sometimes to the embarrassment of their parents. Many persons carry with them the remnants of these early exhibitionistic tendencies, which are shown by attempts to make themselves prominent and to seek the limelight. Parents, however, suppress these tendencies in their children as naughty and revolting, and they even threaten the child bodily harm through punishment if he continues such forms of expression. These tendencies toward exhibitionism are strongest in connection with the genital organs, perhaps because most intense feelings are concentrated in them and also because parental threats are most violent in connection with attempts to expose or display them. This tendency to be interested in the body makes its appearance in later years in many ways. When illness strikes a person, he tends to withdraw his interests from outer affairs and concentrates his attention onto his body. The self-love of a person for his body becomes noticeable in self-concern regarding accidents and injuries. Persons in later life also show it by adornment of the body and by primping. In old age there is frequently a return to interest in the body and a concern with its soundness and freshness. Indeed, there may be a fusion of love for the body and self-punishment. Many persons seem to find intense enjoyment in applying salves and lotions or in taking medicines, while at the same time body infirmities or handicaps have value as forms of self-limitation or punishment.

One who is sensitive to these early forms of narcissism can see their residues in the habits and adjustments of mature people. There are those who go through life expecting favors and depending on others to provide them with pleasures and satisfactions. Somewhere in their early experience these individuals have learned to lean heavily on others for their pleasure. Others indicate the direction their values take by collecting, hoarding, and saving. Many forms of positive feeling and expression of value find their beginning in some infantile process.

In infancy interest is gradually withdrawn from merely gaining satisfactions, and the self becomes a separate object of value, as it were. Little by little, the self takes precedence over other values and goals, and it becomes more cherished and protected than any other single object. The self takes on value in large measure because it is the source of so many satisfactions. As the baby is able to manipulate objects and move about, as he finds in consequence of being a separate self that he can control other persons, and as other persons respond to him as a separate person he begins to find value in himself. The ego not only *acts* and *feels* but also *feels good* or *feels bad* about the self. One has a tendency to applaud oneself when successful and to say not only to others but to oneself, "What a good boy am I!" On the other hand, one has a tendency to berate and scold oneself when one has failed to meet his own expectations, and the self may be hateful—something to be disparaged, condemned, and punished. Gradually distinct emotions are built up around the self as contrasted with those which pertain to others. One can see this clearly in childhood as a child shows signs of jealousy and hurt feelings when attention is given to another child who is a rival. As the self acquires value, the individual is helped to develop prudence and foresight and to check unrestricted expression of the basic drives. One stops eating because one has feelings of satiety, but one may also stop eating in order not to become ill, or in order not to offend one's elders who would call one a pig or glutton. This development of love of the self as a person—primary narcissism—not only gives the self value, but places the self in a vulnerable position, for when one loves, he not only cherishes the loved object but feels hurt if in some way it is damaged or slighted. The very growth which gives the self value may also make it possible for the individual to feel slighted, offended, insulted if in some way he is not given the privileged position or the attention which he craves.

Primary narcissism is concerned only with the self and the advantages it can gain. It is not concerned with others, hence primary narcissism is not concerned with, or related to, good or evil. Moral issues do not arise in connection with primary narcissism, and the individual who regresses to this primitive stage is beyond reach of ethical considerations.

DEVELOPMENT OF SELF-SATISFACTION

Primary narcissism normally reaches its maximum expression in a child from about three to five years. It is at this age that the child is most self-interested, self-willed, and selfish. The child looks on everything and everybody as catering to his pleasure and comfort. At this stage the child has a need to be loved without winning it or deserving it or without giving anything in return. His motives are entirely selfish or egoistic. Children resist giving up their narcissism. They have to be encouraged to share, to go without and to comply, sometimes against considerable resistance. Narcissism is greatest at the very age when the ego itself is least capable of meeting reality and adjusting to it. At the time the child can do least for himself he makes the greatest demands on others. Interference with development at this period may lead to exaggerated narcissistic tendencies in later years.

Narcissism is a term which has been loosely and inexactly used throughout literature, so that several serious inconsistencies have arisen in connection with its use. Probably there are many kinds of self-love, and at least two kinds can be clearly distinguished. One kind is based on parental acceptance. The child who is accepted by his parents tends to feel secure and confident in himself. He has genuine self-esteem, rooted in emotional security and based on a realistic appraisal of the self. This kind of self-love is not dependent on anxiety and, as we shall later see, is the basis of object love; for only as a person genuinely respects himself can he love another person.

The child rejected by his parents is also narcissistic, but in quite a different way. The child who is denied love by his parents is thrown back on himself for love. He is forced to find pleasure in himself rather than in persons and experiences outside and frequently is driven to autoerotic practices in an attempt to derive the pleasure denied him in his contacts with others. Such a person builds a fantasied, instead of a realistic, appraisal of himself. He magnifies himself through day-dreams as he becomes his own hero in fantasied exploits. He becomes aggressive, goaded by the necessity of wresting a good opinion of himself from the outside world by forcible means. His attempt at gaining power is his insurance against the underlying belief in his own unworthiness. Narcissism based on rejection is rooted in emotional insecurity and is tinged with anxiety. The person who is fundamentally unsure of himself but builds himself up in fantasy and in self-stimulation is unfit for social relations with others.

Ordinarily one keeps his ego level as high as possible so that the self shall have some justification for the values which it has set. So it is normal to like oneself and to expect much from oneself. *Self structure* is a term which may be used to designate the pattern of interests and values built up around the self.

Relations Between the Ego and the Self

There are interesting relations between the ego and the self. Awareness of the self keeps pace with the expanding ego. As the ego enlarges its power of perceiving, thinking, and acting, so the self, which is the awareness of this growing capacity for control and adjustment, has more of which to become aware and hence develops concurrently. The concept of the self is determined in large measure by the success or failure of the ego. In striving to *do* one's best in any task or situation one is also striving to *become* one's best, that is, to outdo one's rivals and to assert oneself as superior to them. It is difficult to keep separate ego mastery and the enhancement of the self, as they both ebb and flow in parallel fashion. The successfully functioning ego leads to self-confidence, self-assurance, and self-reliance (126). These qualities are the result of having the ability to meet the demands in time and place as defined by others. When one can function adequately so as to meet the approval of others, then he gains self-esteem and self-confidence.

Hart (104) points out that a certain amount of ego security based on a realistic mastery of oneself in one's surroundings and a realistic self appraisal is necessary for a stable self-valuation. In particular there must be harmony between the ego and superego—one must be oriented to act in directions approved by family, friends, and society at large if one is to feel comfortable with oneself.

On the other hand, success and failure of the ego are to a degree determined by the adequacy of the self, that is, the individual's concept and valuation of himself. Snygg and Combs (192, pp. 78, 219) point out that the self is the core of behavior and all behavior is appropriate to it, or as we would state it, the self is a partial determinant of the ego. Buchenholz and Frank (29) report that in a war trauma, as the individual loses his self-concept, he can no longer react in a routine, integrated and adequate fashion which he developed on the basis of a positive self-valuation, but he retreats to less effective attempts at adjustment.

The ego functions best when the self is valued, whereas

self-depreciation is usually accompanied by a falling off of
the effectiveness of ego functioning. Self-valuation determines
the kind of behavior that will take place (8). It sets the stage
for effective functioning and gives the cue for an output of
energy. When the self is valued behavior becomes more organized, consistent, more forward-moving, more effective,
realistic, and planful.

A child with low self-esteem is actually afraid of the obliga-
tion of living up to praise and of being successful. The person
who believes in himself acts accordingly and puts forth effort
to further his ends; but the person who depreciates himself
sometimes gives up the struggle, and his performance as a
consequence suffers.

The defensive functions of the ego bear an interesting relation to the self inasmuch as they are carried on on behalf of
the self. Defense mechanisms proceed from self-respect and
self-regard. The individual finds the need for building up a
barrier to protect his self-regard and this serves as the motivating force for repression. An individual represses impulses,
because to admit them would tear down the values which he
has built up around the self (18). Rogers (174) points out that
the adequate person is one whose attitudes toward self are
neither emotionally self-depreciative nor emotionally self-
approving but are objective and realistic with a slight tendency to be positive rather than negative. When a person depreciates his own abilities and accomplishments, or when
in fantasy he magnifies his potentialities and believes that he
can accomplish more than he has the capacity for, then disparity between the ego and self becomes a neurotic or even
psychotic adjustment.

Mental health depends in large measure on the degree and
kind of self-valuation (8). It is almost a matter of definition
to say that the mentally healthy person is one who has self-
confidence and self-assurance whereas to lack self-esteem is

one sign of mental illness. The person who is self-confident is free from tensions and feelings of conflict, and freedom from these are considered criteria of good adjustment.

Conditions of Self-Adequacy

Self-esteem is first of all a function of being loved or of gaining the respect of others. It has already been pointed out on pages 75–77 how the concept a person forms of himself is socially determined. A little child also values himself as he is valued by others. When his mother or father speak to him proudly and approvingly and call him a good boy, then he thinks of himself proudly and approvingly. On the contrary, when his parents or teachers criticize and depreciate him he can only think of himself as being unworthy. Self-esteem is lowered when love is lost and when one fails to receive the coveted word of approval. On the other hand, self-esteem is raised when love is regained and when one is applauded and praised.

From the work of Bruner (27, 28) we know that percepts are selected in terms of motivation—we perceive our world in ways to further our purposes. As definitions of the self are gradually built up—the good boy or the bad boy because of this or that characteristic or behavior—they operate to select perceptions of the world which are consistent with these self-concepts. For example, the child whose parents exclaim because he has remembered a number, or was able to do a sum mentally, may find numbers and their manipulation particularly interesting and may notice numbers whenever they come within his field of attention. For him numbers are friendly bits of experience. Those perceptions which do not help us to enhance the self are often not accepted—they are frequently repressed, and to the extent that they are repressed they prevent the ego from fulfilling its integrative functions. So the integrative functions of the ego are largely determined by the integrative character of the concept of the self. If there are areas of the self which we dislike and do not admit as real or true, then we are liable to threats and open to conflict.

This is the point made so tellingly by Lecky (135) with his principle of self-consistency. If there are phases of the self which an individual cannot admit, if he does not believe he has it in him to be musical, or friendly, or wise, then he tends to act in accordance with these beliefs about himself and as a result his ego functioning—his success and adequacy—suffer. Snygg and Combs (192, p. 136), following Rogers (173), have defined the self as adequate "in the degree to which it is capable of accepting into its organization any and all aspects of reality."

According to this point of view no one is ever as adequate as he might be. Everyone has potentialities which he does not dare to admit to himself and everyone carries around with him beliefs in his inadequacy which would evaporate into insignificance and unimportance if all aspects of the self in relation to the world about could be examined openly and frankly.

Self-esteem is also a function of success. De Groot (43), writing from the psychoanalytical point of view, has stated that a satisfying feeling of self-esteem requires a balance between narcissistic (self-love) and aggressive tendencies.

LEVEL OF ASPIRATION

In order to discuss success it is necessary to go into the topic of *level of aspiration,* which has been the subject of considerable psychological investigation. In this area there are many subtle shades of meaning and one must pay close attention to the terms and concepts used in order to understand the relationships which have been discovered. Level of aspiration itself has several shades of meaning. On the one hand, it refers to what one would *like* to do or to be. This may be called the *ideal goal.* One would like to be able to be the bridge champion, the wealthiest man in town, an artist on the violin, even though it is recognized that the chances are remote of ever being able to accomplish these ideal goals. Individuals differ, of course, in the degree to which their ideal goals meet the expectations of reality. Some individuals in fantasy hold unattainable goals while others of a more realistic stamp dare only to look at goals which are within their reach. A second meaning of level of aspiration may refer to what one aims or intends to do which is sometimes called the *action goal.* The action goal is always lower, more or less, than the ideal goal. This action goal may be differentiated in the third place from what one actually *expects* to do, which is not really a goal at all but a judgment as to what one thinks he will actually accomplish.

Experimenters with level of aspiration have evolved several concepts in terms of differences between the level of aspiration and actual accomplishment. The difference between the ideal goal and the action goal, already described, has been called the *inner discrepancy.* The difference between the action goal and the goal of expected performance has been called the *goal expectation discrepancy.* These two concepts, inner discrepancy and goal expectation discrepancy, are measures of differences between the three meanings that may be taken for level of aspiration.

The difference between the action goal and past performance has been called the *goal discrepancy.* If one plans to do better on the next succeeding trial than he did last time the goal discrepancy is positive. If one holds as his goal to do as well as he did last time, the goal discrepancy is zero. If one sets a lower goal than past performance, goal discrepancy is negative. Goal discrepancy is sometimes taken as another meaning of level of aspiration. It is level of aspiration with reference to past performance. *In the following discussion, however, level of aspiration will be used in the sense of the action goal, that is, the goal which the subject intends to reach.*

To go on, the difference between the level of aspiration (the action goal) and performance the next time one tries is called *attainment discrepancy. Attainment discrepancy becomes a measure of success and failure.* Performance which is equal to or even better than the level of aspiration (action goal) we call successful. On the other hand, performance which does not come up to the level of aspiration is called failure. Years ago William James (120) gave as his formula for *self-esteem* that it equals *success* divided by *pretensions.* Here he has somewhat the same meaning as have the modern experimenters with level of aspiration although he has used his terms with a slightly different sense. The modern formula would be *success equals performance divided by pretensions.*

Success and failure, therefore, have a relation to the level of aspiration and are not measured in terms of absolute performance. Success and failure are as much dependent on the level of aspiration as on actual performance. The same performance may be considered a success or a failure according to the level of aspiration. With a high action goal, a given performance may be a failure, but with a low action goal the same performance may be considered a success. If level of aspiration is high, one may have a sense of failure even though by all ordinary standards one has done well. On the other hand, if one's level of aspiration is low, even relatively meager performance may be interpreted as a success. The man who considers himself a top-notch sailor will feel that he has failed even if he comes in second in the cat-boat race, but if he is a novice he may feel the flush of success if he crosses the finish line at all.

But in this respect there are individual differences. Some individuals may have absolute standards for success, but relative standards for failure, while others have relative standards for success but absolute standards for failure. For one person failure means to fail as the school defines it—to receive an F; for another person to fail means to do more poorly than last time. One person is satisfied only with perfection; another is satisfied when he has excelled his classmates or his own past record.

An interesting corollary of this finding is that success and failure may not be experienced at all when performance is very high or very low (113). If the task is too easy (large negative goal discrepancy) and performance is creditable, it may not result in a feeling of success because it is outside of his level of aspiration. One does not feel that he has been successful when he ties his shoe lace, climbs the front steps to his house or raises his glass to his lips because these are so absurdly easy as to lie entirely outside of his level of aspiration. But for a little child just learning to master these skills, performance of them would certainly be felt to be a success. Likewise, if a task is too hard and performance is uncreditable, it may not result in a feeling of failure because again it lies outside the range of his level of aspiration. Few individuals feel that they have failed when they attempt unsuccessfully to play a difficult billiard shot, to balance a ball on the nose, or to put together a radio set. Balancing the ball may be appropriate to a seal whose vestibular apparatus gives the necessary coördination.

Factors Influencing Level of Aspiration. In the first place, one's level of aspiration is determined by his abilities. One tends to set his level of aspiration within a range which is determined by his abilities. Level of aspiration is ordinarily not set below that point about which there is no doubt of the ability to accomplish nor above that which would be entirely outside of one's abilities.

Level of aspiration is adjusted to the degree of success on previous performance (121). After success, that is, a performance which equals or exceeds one's previous goal expectation, there is a tendency to raise the level of aspiration. On the other hand, after failure the level of aspiration is likely to be lowered so as to avoid the threat to self-esteem. This is a general rule which applies in the majority of instances but not without exception. Some individuals in spite of poor performance master the threat to their self-esteem by keeping their ambitions high (70). There are occasions when one does not lower his level of aspiration even after failure nor does one raise his level of aspiration after success, but these are special cases which go contrary to the general rule and which require special explanation. The time-worn adage, "If at first you don't succeed, then try, try again," illustrates the common admission that it is easy to give up after defeat; while the individual who lets some skill such as typing lapse because he now has a secretary and uses the dictaphone illustrates the second point.

Level of aspiration is also influenced by cultural factors. It is determined in part by the standards that one sets for oneself in comparison with one's peers. When one's own self evaluation corresponds with social values behavior will be consistent with the culture. Those who achieve above the average of their group tend to estimate their future performance too low (to have a negative goal discrepancy). Those who achieve below the average of their group, on the other hand, tend to estimate future performance too high (to have positive goal discrepancy). It has been found in school, for instance, that children who have been informed that they stand above the average of their class tend to set their goals with respect to average class performance, which would be lower than their own performance (12). Likewise, children who have been informed that they stand below the average of their class tend to set their goals high under the influence of the class average, for cultural pressures exerted by parents and teachers tend to make failing children set high levels of aspiration.

The frequency with which the level of aspiration is achieved certainly has something to do with the development of feelings of superiority or inferiority. If a person is repeatedly successful he tends to feel superior, but if he fails to come up to his own expectations and the expectations of society he feels inferior. In this connection once a person has attained a high or low place in a group he bases his expectations in the future on his previous standing. Those who excel expect to continue to excel, those who are inferior think of themselves as failures. This is brought home forcefully by the reactions of classes of graduate students. Each member of the class has been accustomed to standing high in his previous classes. Now as members of a highly selected graduate group they compete with others of superior ability and many must, perforce, occupy a middle position. But many rebel against thinking of themselves as average even in a group which offers them real competition and are tortured in attempting to adjust to the situation.

When one looks beyond his own group, however, another set of influences comes into operation. When one compares himself to a superior group there is a tendency to lower his level of aspiration, while in comparing oneself to an inferior group one raises his level of aspiration (34). For example, the child in school who is in a bright section believes that he is a superior individual and accordingly sets his goals high. The child in a dull section, on the other hand, believes that his performance must be inferior and consequently sets his goals low. This tendency to be influenced by the group of which one is a member carries over to the social class in society so that level of aspiration with regard to life goals is determined by the socioeconomic level of one's class.

Level of aspiration is also a function of habitual success or failure (121). Those with habitual failure tend on the average to set higher levels of aspiration (in terms of goal discrepancy) than those with habitual success (187). Those with habitual success, being under no pressure to have to prove themselves, can set their goals very much on the same level as past performance. Those who have failed, however, feel the necessity for greater striving in order to overcome the failure and consequently set their goals higher in relation to past performance. This last statement, however, deserves qualification, for individuals differ in their response to failure. Some individuals who habitually experience failure make strenuous efforts to overcome their deficiency. Others with less of an urge to succeed accept their failure as representing what they can expect of themselves and consequently lower their level of aspiration. The general trend, however, seems to be for those with habitual failure to set their goals somewhat higher.

It is difficult to think of the problem of level of aspiration wholly from the vantage point of the experimental studies which have devoted themselves to this problem because these studies are defined in terms of the limitations of the experimental laboratory, while aspirations penetrate into every corner of living. Actually the level of aspiration of a person refers to the characteristic goals, strivings, and ambitions of the person and the values which are attached to them. When looked at in this way it may be seen that there is not one level of aspiration but many, corresponding to the several goals which a person holds for himself, and to these goals different values are attached which make an individual strive toward them more or less strenuously. However, it may be correct also to think in terms of a general level of aspiration which would be indicated by such comments as, "He is an ambitious person," "He is afraid to exert himself."

Situations apparently similar to an outside observer may

not offer the same intensity of threat of failure to a given individual. It all depends on how he values that activity and whether his performance in it is interpreted by him as important. Gould (98) points out that the individual who is afraid of failing because he wants to succeed has a personality organization which is somewhat different from the person who desires to succeed because he is afraid of failing. Some individuals are more influenced by the possibility of success than by the threat of failure, and vice versa some are more susceptible to the threat of possible failure. Individuals may vary in this according to the nature of the achievement.

Snygg and Combs (192) believe that the goals which we select are related to the concepts which we hold of ourselves. He who values himself highly will strive for high goals while he who has a low opinion of himself will be content with mediocre attainments. Goals are selected because they satisfy the fundamental need to maintain or to enhance the self. Because level of aspiration is thus intimately related to the concept of the self it may be concluded that aspiration is a phenomenon which appears only after the child has acquired some concept of himself and a sense of pride that must be maintained through his endeavors.

Success and failure, then, are functions of self-involvement. Where no goal is set or no aspiration is held there cannot be a feeling of success or failure.

The level of aspiration is highly self-involved (69). This means that level of aspiration is set high when there is some challenge to the self, and the more the self is involved the higher the goal discrepancy with past performance. In addition, the level of aspiration tends to be more constant when the self is involved and is less subject to fluctuation from one task to another (144). Frank (67) believes the evidence points to the goal discrepancy as being a relatively permanent characteristic of personality regardless of the type of task or of the experimental situation. However, Updegraff and Keister (202) report an experiment indicating that young children can be trained to react to failure in more mature ways so that crying and sulking disappear and the child tries longer, shows more interest, and eliminates emotional behavior. It may be added in passing that if a child is easily upset by failure or becomes self-conscious when challenged it indicates the need for training to better forms of adjustment along these lines. Apparently personality organization becomes set and solidified in these respects with increasing years so that adaptability is somewhat lost. On the other hand, without self-involvement, level of aspiration fluctuates according to the nature and difficulty of the task. In the normal person there is a relatively stable relation between the aspiration level and achievement, so that the level of aspiration is set realistically in terms of expected performance. This constant relation between performance and level of aspiration is an important factor in the stable pattern of self-organization.

Goal desires are only one factor determining the level of aspiration score in a laboratory experiment. It is in this connection that Gould (99) has made such an important contribution. Experimenters before her work were quite content to attempt to interpret level of aspiration scores simply as indicating the goals which an individual hoped to attain. These early experimenters overlooked the fact that in even the simplest level of aspiration study the self is involved and an individual responds as much to his need to maintain or enhance himself as to achieve the goal which he sets out for in advance. In no situation which offers a threat of potential failure does one obtain a clear picture of the individual's aspiration level from his aspiration score. The score is always a combination of ambition and the necessity of self-protection.

It is a common observation that an individual may strive mightily for some things and pass others by. One is not able to determine the basic motivations from the extent to which an individual tries in any given situation. One will set a high level of aspiration toward those activities in which the self is highly involved and yet will pass by other activities with no apparent regret. A person who has made a reputation for himself as being an outstanding photographer will permit no picture that he has taken to be displayed unless it comes up to his standards of excellence. On the other hand, the same individual may be sloppy and careless in his clothing because he has never considered it important to find a place on the list of the ten best dressed men. Everyone sets up values within values, and those activities which are considered important may gather value to themselves down to the last detail.

Frank (68), in one of his early papers, states that one may assume that the relation of level of aspiration to past performance depends on the relative strength of a) one's ambitions and the desire to excel and succeed, i.e., the need to keep the level of aspiration as high as possible, b) the need to be realistic, i.e., to make the level of aspiration approximate the level of future performance, and c) desire to avoid failure, i.e., to avoid setting a level of aspiration above future performance. To these Gould (99) adds anxiety and inferiority feelings as determinants of the level of aspiration.

Level of aspiration situations, even in the laboratory, constitute a threat to a person's ability and integrity and bring into play various mechanisms to protect the supreme value of the self. Setting a goal with reference to past performance not only indicates level of aspiration but also serves as a technique to protect the individual from experiencing failure.

In special cases there are many interesting relations between level of aspiration and self-esteem. Some individuals who enjoy the least esteem from others tend to exhibit the most extreme level of aspiration, apparently a compensatory attempt to bolster and protect their own self-esteem. One may suspect that the individual who boasts of his expected performance is the individual who actually feels insignificant and has been treated as insignificant by others.

Discrepancies between aspiration level and performance are sometimes reacted to as incentive and sometimes as failure. Gould (99) found that those individuals for whom there is a wide discrepancy between goal and performance tend to react to the discrepancy as an incentive. However, where the discrepancy is low it more often is reacted to as failure.

In general, performance which is below the standard striven for is reacted to as signifying failure or by disappointment and discouragement, or by making plans to overcome the threat to the self in the future.

Gould (99), by interviewing her subjects, found a variety of reactions to failure or the possibility of failure. Some individuals are stimulated to try to do better when they are faced with failure; others become discouraged and downhearted; others become even more disorganized and confused with regard to the task and their relation to it. Some individuals attempt to overcome discouragement by such devices as making excuses and attempting to rationalize their poor performance, or by thinking of possible successes in the future. Some individuals refuse to hold the backward look and insist on placing the focus of their attention on what they hope to accomplish in the future. Still others react to the situation in more extreme ways. Some lose interest in the task and in the experiment and show signs of wishing to quit; the desire to succeed or to excel fades. Others attempt to compensate for their failure by priding themselves on accomplishments in other directions. Still other individuals manage to dodge the threat of failure by concentrating their attention on certain aspects of the problem. Some compulsive individuals make a game out of the accuracy of their estimates or they may be interested in keeping a record of their performance and treating the results statistically.

The mere statement of a level of aspiration may provide its own satisfaction. Apparently a person feels that he is worth more when he sets his goals and ambitions high, even though he experiences constant failure, than when he lowers his goals in order to be more successful. Some individuals prefer the prestige that comes from being a successful merchant or college professor in a small community (the big fish in the little pond). Others, however, feel a greater sense of personal worth if they continue to struggle unsuccessfully in the face of greater competition in the larger community because they feel that they are competing with more worthy opponents. Some individuals would prefer to be in the lower brackets of the class A tennis tournament than in the higher brackets of the class B tennis tournament.

Level of aspiration is important because it serves as an incentive and carries one on in normal circumstances to higher levels of performance.

Horney (114), as a result of her analytic study of individuals in distress, finds the giving up of pretensions to yield more relief than the gratifying of one's aims. However, most persons cling to their pretensions as a drowning person grasps at the straw.

One interesting study by Escalona (51) suggests that level of aspiration is intimately related to emotional adjustment. In a level of aspiration experiment maladjusted subjects became more emotionally involved, became more helpless, refused to take responsibility for their decisions, and in general found the experiment to be an unpleasant situation.

OTHER CONDITIONS OF SELF-ADEQUACY

This long discussion of level of aspiration concerned the place of success in contributing to self-esteem and self-valuation. Among other factors which enhance self-esteem is the possession of power. Individuals feel that the possession of power over others enhances their own sense of personal worth.

Many persons enhance their self-esteem by superficial means. Dress, for instance, by being modish or ostentatious, helps to enhance self-esteem. Employers have discovered that the uniform when given to the guard, the doorman, the bell-boy, or the elevator operator helps to give added prestige and dignity to the position. Many years ago New York City attempted to raise the morale of street cleaners by insisting that they wear a white uniform (so that they were called "white wings").

Hart (104) discusses compensatory self-esteem, that is, self-esteem that is blown up in order to compensate for ego weak-nesses. He believes that compensatory narcissistic tendencies —relations with other people in order to gain support from them and to inflate one's own self-valuation—are not in them-selves dangerous to mental health, but they point to weak-nesses in ego control and disharmony between the ego and other parts of the personality structure.

Of the many factors that tend to lower self-esteem, only one will be mentioned here—guilt. Guilt, the form of anxiety at failing to meet standards which one sets for oneself, tends to lower self-esteem just as success tends to raise it.

Another factor contributing both positively and negatively to self-esteem is love. Actually when one gives his love to another person there is a depletion of self-valuation. The lover traditionally feels unworthy and tends to belittle himself in favor of his beloved. However, self-esteem comes back with a rush as it is enriched by the gratification of love returned. Mutual love tends to enhance the self-esteem of both parties as they support each other in their mutual affection.

Recent discussions have emphasized that self-valuation is to a large extent socially determined. One values oneself in proportion to values that are expressed toward the individual by the group. As an individual is praised by his group and is selected by it to be the leader or the representative, that individual feels himself enhanced and more confident. One values himself in terms of the group norms and group expectations. In a society in which aggression is the group norm, an individual who displays his aggression thereby enhances his self-esteem, but in a society where aggression if frowned upon the aggressive individual finds that his self-esteem is lessened.

As one approaches maturity his self-values are determined increasingly by the opinions held of him by his age-mate group as contrasted with opinions expressed in earlier years by his elders. Self-values are a function of status values. If one's status in his group is respected, then the self feels assured and confident; but if one is an outcast or is under suspicion by his group, then inevitably doubts begin to rise in his mind concerning his own self-value, and his self-esteem is lowered. An individual can maintain his self-esteem in the face of ostracism only when he has inner values that transcend the values of his group. This happens sometimes when religious teachings go against the common mores of society and an individual is bulwarked by what he believes to be true in opposition to the standards generally accepted about him.

Threat to the Self

Snygg and Combs (192) have elaborated the concept of threat to the self which originated in the work of Rogers and his students. According to these authors the self is threatened when concepts of the self become inconsistent, that is, when there is conflict between different phases of the personality and when the self has lost its integrated character. For instance, there is a threat to the self when, on the one hand, one thinks of himself as being strong, effective, and self-sufficient, and on the other hand, as being weak and ineffective. A woman, for instance, likes to think of herself as being an efficient housekeeper, a loving and dutiful wife, a good mother, a powerful force for community betterment; but there are times when doubts cross her mind, particularly when disagreements arise between herself and her husband and when her son fails to make a good record in school and has difficulty in his relationships with other boys. Her vision of herself as an efficient person is suddenly threatened and the edifice of the self which she believed to be so strong threatens to crumble.

A high-school boy who has grown up in a family where sex has been minimized and where affection is expressed by the merest glance or smile finds when he reaches high school that he is expected to "pet" when he goes out with a girl. This new social expectation runs in conflict with the picture of himself which he has developed from the patterns of behavior in his own family. The expectancy of his own group constitutes a threat and he must find some way of reconciling himself to the new standards.

In general, inconsistent concepts may not both be conscious at the same time. Ordinarily we maintain our integrity by holding only one picture of ourselves before us and repressing all other pictures. If, by chance, the concept of our self which we ordinarily hold becomes threatened, it arouses anxiety and produces discomfort. When one concept of the self is repressed, the potentialities of threat are constantly present, and to the extent that the repressed concept is considered bad, wicked, or dangerous, the potentialities of threat are tremendous.

One can well understand why one clings to a positive concept of the self, but it becomes more difficult to understand why an individual should persist in thinking of himself as being inadequate, ineffective, inept or stupid. To hold such attitudes toward the self indicates a masochistic tendency. A person does not dare to think well of himself for fear that such a concept would be toppled and then he would be disgraced in his own sight. He prefers to look at himself modestly, probably always keeping in the background of consciousness vague ideals and aspirations which he would gladly accept if they could be accepted safely and without challenge.

Threat is at a maximum when the self is perceived as being inadequate to deal with events and situations that are daily met. The threat remains as long as either of two conditions persist: (a) as long as the self is defined as inadequate, or (b) as long as the challenge to the effectiveness of the self remains in the field. We are threatened if we feel inadequate to meet the challenge of the coming examination for which we do not feel fully prepared, and as long as the examination still is before us in time.

Threats to the self lead to self-defense, or to a need to enhance and build up the self. Threats to the self have a restrictive effect upon the field of perception. When we feel threatened our attention narrows and we confine our interest to the situation with which we are confronted. Snygg and Combs call this "tunnel vision," an apt expression which vividly describes what apparently takes place. Under threat, confusing and interfering points of view are repressed. Perceptions which threaten the self cannot be accepted in the organization of personality. Each of us has a tendency to build ourselves up and to look for those aspects of ourselves with which we can feel most comfortable and which help to raise morale.

Failure to accept a perception, however, does not eliminate the threat. To the extent that the threat is based on unconscious forces which are found difficult to accept, these forces are ever threatening to press their way into the field of consciousness and consequently the threat of them is constantly present. Ordinarily threat leads to an increase in energy output, and under threat an individual becomes tense, hurried, and restless.

Self-Defense

Because the self is prized so highly the ego takes strenuous measures to protect the self from threats to its status or to enhance its status. Many of the defense mechanisms have as their main purpose maintaining the integrity of the self.

A common method of maintaining the self is to turn on one's attackers aggressively. Many forms of aggression are really attempts to anticipate attacks from others in an effort to forestall them and thereby to maintain one's own prestige. Early psychoanalytic discussions of aggression pointed out its sexual basis. However, more recent developments lend credence to the belief that aggression is principally in the defense of the self. Many forms of aggression show that they are self-involved. In projected aggression there is an attempt to focus the attention on the possibility of attack from without, blinding oneself to one's own need to retaliate or destroy. The little child's negativism and resistance to the wishes of his parents are the beginnings of his attempts to throw a barrier around the first manifestations of his self-valuation in order to protect it from assault and injury. Just because the two-year-old is tiny and helpless he resists his parents in order to gain a degree of self-respect and autonomy. Jealousy in an older child also is a sign of the struggle to maintain his place in the family situation. With older children competition is an aggressive attempt to meet the challenge of a threat to self-esteem.

Turning away the gaze in the presence of a person who threatens by his dominance may be a method of preventing an invasion of the self by others who may wish to dominate him.

Methods of defending the self against attacks on one's prestige may in the long run defeat their own ends. The individual may overdo his efforts at defense and cut off his own nose to spite his face. For instance, face-saving may be contrary to one's best interests. In order to protect one's prestige one may limit his spontaneity or cut himself off from profitable undertakings. The "proper Bostonian" who feels the necessity of protecting his family name may cut out from his life many of the satisfactions which individuals in a freer and more spontaneous society enjoy. Face-saving is highly developed among the orientals who will go to great lengths to maintain their prestige and dignity even though it means forfeiting favorable contracts. Sometimes an individual feels that he must defend himself against the very things that might help to improve or enhance his station. When a person has been insulted his first impulse may be some form of retaliation even though the person who made the insult really needs to be courted because through him certain advantages can be gained. It is too easy to take the short-sighted view and to attempt to preserve one's dignity in the present without forethought as to what one might become in the future. It is probably to the advantage of self-interest on many occasions to humble oneself so that one may have the opportunity to learn and to save and thereby build oneself up to take a higher position in the future (149).

Self-Enhancement

Not only does one attempt to protect the self from ignominy and defeat but there is an attempt to enhance the self and to raise one's own self-esteem. The ego attempts to subsume the most powerful prototypes. There is an attempt to be superior, good, masculine, free, potent, beautiful, wealthy, fast, tall, and strong. Each of these and others besides represent the ideal goals of a considerable part of human striving. A common way of enhancing the self is by identifying oneself with the admired person. A boy may copy the clothing or stance of his baseball hero, the girl may copy the hair-do or gesture of the photographer's model whose charm and notoriety she secretly admires.

Those individuals who have a need to enhance themselves sometimes attach a morbidly intense value to the self. When the self is inflated in value and one goes about continually boasting, claiming possession of extraordinary talents, or bragging of one's prowess and exploits, one is forestalling doubts that one has with regard to weaknesses in other directions.

In our culture, at least, the self is a competitive entity. One attempts to enhance the self by demonstrating that he is superior to others. The self is moved upwards by fierce competition in business, in sports, in appearance, in morality, in fact in every phase of life. Much that looks like competition for objects is actually competition for status. The competition for the prize or the honor is actually an attempt to enhance the self in comparison with others. As one matures and defines his goals more clearly and develops goal-seeking techniques, he also perfects his techniques in competition. Adolescence is the period when goals should become clarified and methods of achieving these goals be worked out through the competitive struggle.

One of the methods employed is that of extending the boundaries of the self so as to include wider interests. Establishing effective and helpful relationships with other people is a form of insurance. The wider the interests with which the self is concerned, the more one has to fall back on in case any one interest should fail. The larger the family, the wider the estate, the more enterprises in which one may be engaged,—all these serve in bolstering up the sense of one's own value and make barricades against failure and loss (149).

Many persons find social activities, such as belonging to an organization, with the status that is carried with them, help to enhance the self, and this may be one of the principal values in joining a fraternal order.

The self may also be enhanced by physical culture, for a well-functioning physical apparatus leads to feelings of well-being and self-satisfaction. The boy may take up strenuous exercise or cold baths to toughen his muscles or to harden himself, while the girl may reduce her weight to attain a willowy figure or use cosmetics to accentuate the features which she believes bring her admiration. Clothing is chosen very largely not for warmth or protection but to enhance the self.

Much has been said about "defense mechanisms." The so-called defense mechanisms are really self-defense mechanisms and oftentimes their purpose is as much self-enhancement as it is a defense against those forces which might destroy self-esteem. Most of the mechanisms result in a kind of self-deception which seems to be necessary in order to maintain, enhance, and restore the self. Repression is necessary for most persons so that they can keep their dignity and self-esteem. Rationalization, denial, and projection all help the individual to avoid facing unpleasant facts about himself.

The individual is constantly on the alert to protect himself from threat or to raise his own self-esteem,[2] and to the extent that he can perceive threats or opportunities for self-enhancement, he will act on them. It happens, however, that behavior designed to enhance one aspect of the self may give rise to additional threats. When an individual strives to better his position by strenuous efforts he may find he has aroused the

[2] Tendencies toward self-punishment and self-depreciation would seem to contradict this statement, but such tendencies may only disguise hidden tendencies beneath. Just as a parent may punish a child with the hope that the child will mend his ways, so an individual may adopt masochistic tendencies in order to reap a greater reward eventually. The statement should be corrected to read, "The individual is constantly on the alert to protect himself from threat or to raise his own self-esteem except when for special masochistic reasons he finds a need to humiliate himself and to compromise his interests."

envy and hostility of his colleagues. Many a factory worker has been prevented from outdistancing his fellow workers by the restraint of those whose position might thereby be threatened.

Frequently efforts at self-enhancement in one direction mean the abandonment of efforts in another direction, or an oscillation between the two. Efforts to achieve may be a threat to health. Attention to the culture of the body may take time from one's business pursuits. In the complex world in which we live today it is absolutely necessary to choose between goals.

Too intense value placed on the self may interfere with the relation between basic drives, external reality, and the superego (164). As self-esteem is heightened an individual may release some of his inhibitions and self-restrictions. Success frequently opens forbidden outlets and there is relaxation of inner controls. While some who achieve wealth are never able to drop their earlier habits of thrift, the excesses of the *nouveau riche* are notorious. Even Noah, after his self-discipline in building the ark and carrying all of its inhabitants through the flood, relaxed after the strain was over and got drunk (Genesis 9:21). It is common observation that the nation which has girded itself up to a high degree of self-discipline during periods of national emergency will relax its self-imposed discipline when the emergency is over. But relaxation may arouse guilt and lead to a reaction which is more repressive than was the original condition.

Some Implications of Self-Value

A term which has come into common usage in psychology is "ego involvement" (119). The origin of the use of this term is shrouded in obscurity. Apparently it was used in discussions among psychologists before it appeared in print. The first use of it in print that can be found is by Frank (68), who connects it with his analysis of level of aspiration. In 1935 he wrote, "It is suggested that the size of the difference between the average level of aspiration and the median level of past performance is due to the involvement of the ego-level of the individual in the task, as shown by self-assertion or social pressure." Klein and Schoenfeld (126) used the term in 1940 in the title of a report of an experimental investigation, "The Influence of Ego-Involvement on Confidence." In the same year, Cantril [3] in a discussion of the conditions of suggestibility stated: "Another determinant of the extent to which this condition of suggestibility will hold in any given instance is, as we have stated before, the personal significance of the frames of reference, the degree to which the values from which they are derived involve the ego."

In the terminology of this book this term should be self-involvement. Involvement means very much the same as the Freudian term "cathexis," that is, placement of interest and value on definite objects and persons. Self-involvement means placement of interest and value on the self. This involvement of self leads to a number of well-defined phenomena. For instance, self-value involves one's judgment and attitudes and relations with the world.

The self is involved principally when its security is threatened, that is, when it is subject to attacks or depreciation. The self is also involved when friends, superiors, servants, family, school, church, club, or flag are threatened, when their prestige is challenged, or when they are subject to loss or depreciation (191). What one accomplishes by his own labor is likely to be self-involved, that is, to be of greater value to an individual than that which comes without his efforts. If one wishes to help another person gain self-respect, he can accomplish this most effectively by helping the other person become self-supporting, both psychologically and economically. Charity

[3] Hadley Cantril, *The Psychology of Social Movements* (New York: John Wiley and Sons, Inc., 1941), p. 73.

is seldom self-involved, and what a person receives as a gift may be only partially appreciated.

One's identifications indicate the nature of one's self-involvements. The goal that one sets, the patterns that one follows, the ideals that one upholds indicate where one's self-interests lie.

However, only a part of the culture is self-involved for a given individual at any time (8). One's interests do not turn in all directions. Even the most highly developed individual can spread his interests only so far and fight for only a limited number of causes. Likewise only certain emotional states are self-involved. Many things happen to us which we do not take too personally. There are only certain emotional states in which we feel ourselves to be personally implicated (8). The wealthy man may contribute liberally to the Boy Scout organization because he has nostalgic memories of his own scouting activities, but he may be unsympathetic with and unresponsive to equally meritorious causes and charities because they do not touch him personally at any point.

Kris (131) has pointed out that laughing at the comic is a sure sign that one is concerned with success or failure. Most situations become comic because the self is involved in them. Without this self-involvement the comical aspects of situations simply do not appear. What one laughs at is what one feels safe in having avoided or what one is secretly striving to achieve.

Some interesting and clear-cut findings growing out of investigations of phenomena to be found in nondirective therapy indicate that there is a distinct relationship between the way a person feels about himself and the way he feels about others. Sheerer (188) and Stock (196) have demonstrated a correlation between attitudes of acceptance and respect for self and attitudes of acceptance and respect toward others. The more a person esteems himself, the more he tends to esteem others.

One can be fairly sure that the person who is critical of others sets a low valuation on himself in spite of assertions to the contrary, and vice versa the person who esteems his fellows really thinks well of himself.

Social attitudes require a certain degree of self-development, for social attitudes help to define a person's status and hence are self-involved. One cannot take an attitude toward social issues without at the same time involving himself actively in those issues, and hence he cannot take a positive stand for or against until there is a self that cares and is concerned.

Self values also determine our loyalties and our obligations. The martyr who sacrifices himself for a cause, even to the extent of harming his interests in other directions, illustrates the directing and limiting effect of self-involvement. Self-value, in part, determines rôle, status, and class (191). One plays a given rôle (good citizen, good parent, good church member) so long as it continues to furnish him with satisfaction and self-enhancement. Self-involved attitudes, that is, attitudes in which we care about the outcomes, guide us in our thoughts and actions as we try to maintain or improve our status or as we try to shift our status with changing conditions.

If a given group or class satisfies the basic needs of the self for an individual, then he becomes a responsible group member. If the labor union promises to increase one's economic position, the worker becomes a loyal member. So one's class membership is determined by the self-values which it enhances, and the individual's self-esteem is consolidated by the group to which he adheres. If basic needs are not satisfied by group membership, then some other adjustment is required (191). A considerable part of self-striving is an attempt to make one's status or position in the group secure.

The intensity of motivation is a function of self-value.

When one engages in a task in which he is personally interested and involved, he will expend more energy than when he engages in a task which is set for him by someone else and for which he will gain at best only some extrinsic reward. This is the distinction between intrinsic and extrinsic motivation.

Recent experiments have also indicated that perception, judgment, learning, and memory are to a considerable extent self-involved. The ways in which we perceive our world is a function of the way in which we appraise ourselves. If we think of ourselves as successful then we may approach the world benignantly, but if we think of ourselves as failures then suspicion and distrust of others may prevail. Our evaluation of ourselves may also affect bodily processes as recent studies in psychosomatic medicine have demonstrated so graphically. Under self-involvement, that is, when the person cares, the speed of learning is superior than when the person does not care. It has also been demonstrated that retention is superior when the individual cares to remember, when it is to his interest to do so, and when he makes an effort to remember (11). Tresselt and Levy (201) have demonstrated that recognition memory is superior when it is self-involved. Lewin and Zeigarnik (139) discovered many years ago that incompleted tasks are recalled more easily than completed tasks. However, later experiments have not verified in every instance this earlier finding. Apparently the retention and recall of incompleted tasks is a function of one's self-involvement in the task. When the goal is the completion of the task which otherwise means very little to the individual there is a greater recall of the task when it is incomplete, and when it is completed, it is easily forgotten. However, when the task is self-involved there is greater recall if it is a completed task; that is, the individual feels proud of his accomplishment and takes pleasure in recalling it, whereas a task on which the person has failed is a threat to his prestige and this is more quickly forgotten (139, 175).

Allport also believes that, as a factor in determining learning, considerations of self-involvement take precedence over the law of effect, which states that those reactions followed by satisfaction tend to be repeated and hence to be learned. According to Allport, this law operates only in those situations in which it was discovered experimentally, that is, with animals and with man in situations in which he is not too concerned about the outcome. When a man is concerned about the outcome it is seldom that he repeats a successful performance—rather he turns his attention to other tasks. It is probably true, as Thorndike found, that, with a given goal in mind, satisfaction and success may serve to guide the individual in the choice of responses to be repeated and to be eliminated. According to Allport, effect becomes only one of the factors in the perceptive situation which the individual may use in determining his course of action, and that at bottom the determining factor in the choice of behavior is the enhancement and defense of the self (10, 147, 171).

Thorndike (199) believed that the law of effect is operative in determining wants, interests, and attitudes, but his experiments concerned attitudes which were not highly self-involved. The upshot of this discussion is to cause a revision in the concept of "effect" so as to include the enhancement and protection of the self among the more important satisfactions.

It has been noted that repression is greater under self-involvement. Those things are repressed about which an individual feels ashamed and sensitive. Where an individual does not care, the motive for hiding and covering up an act is weaker. To be able to accept and tolerate repressed material does not mean, however, that these recalled memories are less self-involved. It means that by achieving greater security and through a more highly integrated ego organization the individual is better able to tolerate and accept that which was formerly dangerous and threatening to the self.

Likewise rationalization may be greater under self-involvement, as one finds it necessary to hatch up reasons and excuses which permit him to continue to overlook his real underlying motives.

Changes in Self

This chapter will close with a brief discussion of some of the factors which are involved in changes in the self. In general a person who is satisfied with himself does not change. This follows the same pattern that a person adopts with regard to anything which he values. This statement, too, has its notable exceptions when masochistic tendencies interfere with normal and natural restrictions. What we value we tend to prize and cherish, to preserve and keep. So the self of a satisfied person tends to be a stable organization and in general, as long as a person feels adequate and maintains self-esteem, he retains his personality structure.

The adoption of new self values is frequently upsetting because in some way they become a threat to the continuity and integrity of the self. Most persons feel that their concepts of themselves would tumble if they relaxed their grip on established self-values. A consistent picture of the self is necessary for security, and most persons, in order to avoid anxiety, resist change. One of the stumbling blocks to effective psychotherapy is this tendency of most individuals to resist change in their self structure.

Changes in the self result from failure, unhappiness, feelings of inadequacy and inferiority, doubt, perplexity, and indecision. In some instances the real situation may have changed, leaving behind disparity between the concept of the self and the new situation. A New Englander, accepting a position in a Texas community, probably feels bewildered because the customary reticence and reserve to which he is accustomed are not present and in their stead is to be found outgoingness and spontaneity in human relations. At first the situation arouses conflict and distress. However, if the individual is to adjust to his new surroundings he must find a new concept of himself in relation to the people with whom he must live and work. Sometimes changes in the self are stimulated by inconsistent concepts of the self. One may not live up to his own ideals, for instance, and either he must find ways of incorporating greater discipline into his living or he must be willing to relax his ideals to fit in with his wishes and desires, stimulated by what he sees about him. The person, for instance, who has been brought up in a strict religious home eventually must either find ways of justifying his behavior to himself in the light of the many ways in which the behavior of those about him diverge, or he must acquiesce to the relaxing of the standards which he was taught in his childhood. Most individuals find ways of reconciling and compromising between conflicting demands in our modern society.

So a change in the self depends on an individual's capacity to perceive a difference between his concept of himself and the demands of the situation, particularly the expectations of those about him as they respond to his behavior. If an individual is impervious to the expectations of others, then he will not be particularly disturbed and he will be able to keep himself inviolate, but to the extent that he is sensitive to the expressions of approval or disapproval of others he must modify himself to conform with these expressions.

Snygg and Combs (192, p. 93) say that the ability to perceive the difference between the self and the demands of the situation is dependent upon the ability to see oneself as others see him. However, this is only a partial way of looking at the matter and neglects the inner forces which prevent a clear perception of self-inadequacy. These authors place everything on a conscious level without apparently recognizing that individuals frequently rationalize in order to defend themselves against becoming aware of unconscious motives which they are not able to face directly. Many individuals are unable to form a clear impression of themselves because of their need to justify rather than to understand their behavior. A man may know that he has perfectionistic tendencies and he may be aware that they are criticized by others, but he may attempt to justify them on the grounds of greater efficiency, without recognizing that he would be afraid of the criticism that might be leveled at him were he to do a half-way job. A man may know that he tends to be retiring but justify it on the grounds of being busy and preferring to do things alone, without recognizing that he fears competition and struggle lest others outsmart him or turn the fury of their rivalry upon him.

Changes in the self occur only as a result of experiences. Usually these changes take place exceedingly gradually. It is only as a result of repeated experiences that most individuals gradually become aware of the fact that they are not performing at their highest efficiency, that they are failing to enter into the spirit of the group in which they live, that they are being criticized by their fellows, or that they are hiding unacceptable trends from themselves. Occasionally, however, a change may take place suddenly when an individual has a traumatic experience which forces him with abruptness to face the fact that he is inadequate or out of step with his fellows, and something drastic must be done to remedy the situation.

The closer a deviant perception of the self is to the core of the concept of the self, the more difficult it is to change the self concept. Some aspects of the self are more easy to change than others. In general, those concepts which were formed earliest lie closer to the center of personality and hence are the most difficult to change. Most of us would find it exceedingly difficult to change our sex rôle from male to female, or vice versa, or to change our name, race, religion, membership in a social class, and the like. When a young man is first embarking upon a career he finds it fairly easy to change from one job to another. As he becomes older and established, he finds it more difficult to think of himself in a rôle other than the one he is accustomed to—carpenter, lawyer, merchant, or professor. The boy who volunteers to be the bat boy in a scrub baseball game may feel little threat in relinquishing that position, but the child who is the favored and only son in a family is challenged to the very core of his personality when another sibling arrives.

Individuals under threat sometimes find it difficult to change themselves. A threat seems to arouse defensive processes and the first defenses are thrown up to protect the self. An individual whose status is threatened runs to his own defense and throws his energy into the protection of his status. In general, change in the self is easier when there is an absence of threat. Under threat, perceptions are narrowed and repressed and it becomes difficult for the person to form new perceptions of himself, for he tends to select his perceptions in terms of his previous concepts of himself. This has been recognized in the practice of psychotherapy, and the counselor is advised to eliminate threat by adopting an accepting attitude toward the client. Acceptance by the counselor permits a client freedom to examine and to differentiate all aspects of himself with respect to the surrounding situation. With this freedom the individual is more likely to perceive other aspects of himself and to be able and willing to shift his values and to adopt a new concept of himself.

Sheerer (188) and Stock (196) have found from their studies that a change in the attitude toward the self is correlated with a change in attitude toward others. During psychotherapy, at the same time that an individual is able to accept himself more completely he adopts a more tolerant and appreciative attitude toward others. One may assume that under provocation the opposite process takes place and that as an individual feels himself to be less worthy and less adequate he also becomes more critical and fault-finding of others. There is an intimate relation between the attitude we take toward ourselves and that which we adopt toward the world about us.

7

EGO STRENGTH AND EGO WEAKNESS

The concepts of ego strength and ego weakness have recently come into prominence in connection with the growing interest in personality development and psychotherapy. Ego strength is defined simply as the efficiency of the ego in regulating impulses and mastering the environment. Or to give it a somewhat different emphasis, ego strength is the capacity for sustaining emotional equilibrium while waiting or working for later gratification.

Criteria of Ego Strength

The concept of ego strength is somewhat loose, as will be seen by the following criteria that have been proposed as measures of ego strength. In the first place, by ego strength is meant the capacity to react successfully to environmental stress either by avoiding (repressing) similar experiences or preferably by reacting successfully to them. It is well known that individuals differ in their ability to tolerate threats, deprivations, and traumatic experiences. One individual may be overwhelmed by a loss or a disappointment which another person takes quite in his stride. This concept of ego strength was demonstrated very clearly during the recent war when it was found that some men could not tolerate the discomforts of army life while others not only accepted the rigors of army life but also the hazards of the battle front without emotional disturbance.

A second criterion of ego strength is the development of the synthetic functions of the ego (153). The ego that has found a working relationship between the demands of inner drives, outer demands, and superego requirements is considered stronger than the ego that is filled with conflicts. The ego that has to expend energy to master its drives or to tolerate the criticisms of the superego or the rebelliousness of split-off portions of the ego is naturally restricted in its emotional life and in its ability to approach situations rationally. One can test the synthetic stability of the ego by noting the methods which an individual employs in dealing with feelings of guilt. Where guilt is mastered by too much self-punishment and self-restriction the ego shows less strength than when guilt is reduced or avoided by working out effective compromise between the various demands.

A third criterion of ego strength is the capacity for effective repression. Ability to control impulses and excitement, instead of being a measure of ego weakness as many individuals believe, is actually a sign of ego strength. A good measure of this criterion of ego strength is the capacity of the ego to accept repressed material as it is brought to the consciousness in psychoanalysis. Where repressed material arouses too much anxiety and too strong defenses against this anxiety the ego shows its weakness. The analyst may test ego strength by trial interpretations in order to see how much anxiety or guilt the ego can tolerate when it is aroused by having unconscious processes pointed out to him.

A further criterion of ego strength is to be found in the degree of rigidity as contrasted with the plasticity and elasticity of the personality. Optimum ego strength is somewhere between brittle and rigid adjustment on the one hand, and extremely plastic adjustment on the other. The strong individual is one who has achieved a certain stability of adjustment, but not to the extent that it becomes rigid, blind, and intolerant. On the other hand, ego strength also implies a certain mild degree of elasticity to changing demands, but not to the extent that it gives way impulsively to every demand put upon it. To test the ego strength of a child one may place him in an unfamiliar group of children and note how readily and easily he adapts himself to the individuals in the group.

A fifth criterion of ego strength is found in the ego's ability to live by planned resolutions and compacts with the self. The person of strong ego is one who is able to live up to a self ideal which he has made very much his own. He is the person who can make resolutions and carry them out, whose New Year's resolutions are not flouted before the end of the day, who can adopt a plan of action for himself and not be diverted until he has carried the plan to completion.

A sixth criterion of ego strength may be found in the degree of genuine self-regard. The individual who holds a high opinion of himself and who is free of feelings of inadequacy and inferiority shows greater ego strength than the person who doubts his own capacity and his acceptance by others.

Ego strength cannot be measured in terms of the mechanisms (95). Every individual must adopt certain mechanisms by which he avoids anxiety and keeps himself on an even keel. While it is true that certain mechanisms are considered more constructive than others, by and large, one should not measure ego strength by the form of behavior adopted but by the various signs which have already been mentioned.

Factors Determining Ego Strength

Ego strength is, in the first place, a function of the strength of drive, a fact which is too easily overlooked or forgotten. One's ego depends, in part, on the strength of one's urges and needs, for it is these forces which determine the original development and shape of the ego structure. Were the individual to have no needs or no driving forces, no ego development would take place. Successfully to gratify and to harness strong urges requires a stronger ego organization than to manage drives that are weak.

Just as the self takes on value as it feels loved and respected, so the ego gathers strength as it is loved and respected (59). The child that is loved is most favorably placed for establishing a strong ego, whereas the child who is neglected or hated is forced to devote so much energy toward attaining security that the ego remains weak and undeveloped.

There is some question as to the extent to which displacements contribute to ego strength. On the one hand, as has already been pointed out, the most favorable condition for ego development is one in which the child is helped to accept both his feelings of love and hate toward the same person. However, it is well known that too strong ambivalent trends may be disrupting, and ego strength may be aided if these conflicting trends can be dispersed. This can be accomplished by displacing hostility away from those who are closest to the young child, onto siblings, playmates, and in general a wider circle of individuals. As feelings are thus displaced and also dispersed, it is possible that the ego is thereby enabled to adjust more effectively to reality and gathers strength by this success (95).

Ego gains strength also as libidinal components find expression through such mechanisms as sublimation and reaction formation. Sublimations, on the one hand, help the growing child to find outlets for its activities in socially acceptable ways which bring it in closer touch with reality, and reaction formations aid in repressing socially unacceptable trends. Both of these mechanisms therefore aid in the development of ego strength.

The point has been made that the development of ego strength is conditioned in part by the sequence of experiences. If the growing child is encouraged to self-expression and self-assertion so that he achieves a certain feeling of mastery, he is in a better position to accept frustration and disappointment than if frustration comes before he has gained a feeling of confidence (119). Likewise ego strength is aided if the problems which a child must learn to master are not overwhelming but are those which he can learn to solve. On the other hand, if a child is overwhelmed by situations for which he can find no solution, then the ego remains weak and undeveloped. Parents and teachers should exercise care not to attempt to make the child grow up before he is ready, but should try as far as possible to confront him with tasks and responsibilities in which he can become successful.

Narcissism or self-love also helps to strengthen the ego (153). It has already been pointed out that ego strength is coördinate with self-respect, self-esteem, and self-confidence. One of these feeds into the other, and as the child is helped to become successful and is praised for his efforts his ego gathers strength. The ego becomes strong again when there is optimum freedom from anxiety and guilt. As will be shown later, a certain amount of anxiety is necessary for ego development, but too intense anxiety is crippling (94).

The ego is helped to become strong as it is liberated from a tyrannical conscience. Where the conscience is unduly demanding and threatening and guilt surges up at acts which are contrary to one's standards, the ego is severely tried. To the extent that the superego is reasonable and mild the ego is enabled to work out its relations with the world of reality more effectively and aggressively.

Ego strength is also helped through identifications. A boy is fortunate who has a strong but sympathetic father with whom he can identify. Likewise the girl is helped in forming a strong ego through identification with a mother who is gentle, loving, yet firm. If the parental images are deflated early through disappointment, neglect or cruelty, the ego of the child is left without adequate support and the many problems confronting the child tend to overwhelm him. Likewise ego strength is aided by a strong society, that is, one which is stable and devoted to the interests of its members. In such a society individuality also flourishes. The American ego is strong relatively to that in less democratic societies because our nation has established a stable and secure society.

Ego strength is aided by the integration of early ego nuclei (95). As a family works together as a harmonious unit and parents hold common ideals the child is helped to pull together his reactions to varying experiences into a coördinated team. Likewise ego strength is fostered by lack of contradictions in society. A stable society helps in the development of a strong ego, whereas a rapidly changing society or a society cut up into warring elements such as disparate classes, political parties, or ideologies must split the ego of each individual member apart and contribute to its weakness.

Another factor that may determine the strength of the ego is the child's opportunity to work out experiences through play and sublimation. The child that can experiment actively with situations it is forced to endure passively is the child who is developing ego strength to meet these experiences (153). In play therapy a child is given an opportunity to express himself with regard to family relationships and through this spontaneous activity is enabled easily and quickly to gather ego strength which enables him to meet situations which formerly were overwhelming. Every child needs an opportunity to try out, in fantasy-like play, methods of meeting emotional situations for which he has no adequate response.

Finally, the ego is strengthened nightly through sleep (54).

Whereas fatigue may reduce control and repression, the restoration that occurs during sleep enables the ego to meet the experiences of the next day with greater adequacy.

Factors Contributing to Ego Weakness

It is not necessary to make a detailed rehearsal of the many factors which may contribute to ego weakness, particularly those which are the negative of the ones that have just been recounted as contributing to ego strength. Where any of these factors are missing or expressed in the opposite fashion they constitute threats to ego strength. However, a number of factors that contribute to ego weakness may be briefly mentioned. Among them are various physical factors including fatigue, intoxication, sickness, exacting tasks, and increased sensitivity to pain. Intoxication, whether through drugs or excitement, tends to release inhibitions and deprive the individual of ego control. Sickness, particularly when the child becomes bedridden, places deprivations on a child which may be more than can be tolerated (153). Consequently parents are inclined to indulge the sick child and deprive him of methods of meeting situations through his own efforts.

Any traumatic experience is likely to threaten ego strength. Bettelheim (21) has shown how the ego broke down and disintegrated in Nazi prison camps. Buchenholz and Frank (29) have painted a graphic picture of how, under the stress of continued air raids over enemy territory, the ego strength of aviators was sapped, leading to war neuroses.

Any experience which causes an arrest of development will likewise contribute to ego weakness. Not only is development arrested by such constitutional factors as congenital deformity, birth injury, or feeblemindedness, and by functional physical traumas such as disease, accident, and injury, but of similar importance are those arrests of development which come about through traumatic shifts in personal relations, such as

death or absence of a member of a family or the break-up of
a family. Whenever a child fails to work through satisfactorily
some stage in infantile development he carries with him residues of these unsuccessful infantile strivings which may
threaten the strength of the ego throughout life (153). The
child, for instance, who has never been allowed to work
through his desires to play with dirt may have to struggle with
attitudes toward cleanliness and order throughout life. Where
a child does not have the opportunity of free play and motor
expression which enables him to gain active mastery over his
surroundings he may be destined to reinforce his ego strivings
throughout life by reliance on assistance from other individuals.

Snygg and Combs (192, p. 140) emphasize that threats to
the self help to make the self unchanging and unchangeable
and hence brittle, and this leads to ego inadequacy and in-
effectiveness. The person who persists in thinking of himself
as ineffective must carry over this concept of himself into
action.

A disturbed ego synthesis is a very weak support in ego
structure. Where there are competing elements within that
have never established harmonious working relations there
is danger of increased readiness for anxiety, neurotic reactions,
and crippling feelings of guilt. The disruptive factors which
may affect the integrative functions of the ego may stem from
the basic drives or the superego or from both pulling at cross
purposes.

Likewise the child who is continually bolstered by over-
indulgent or overanxious parents fails to learn how to take
care of himself. If parents cannot afford to give a child the
freedom to explore and learn for himself even at the expense
of mild danger, that child is handicapped in learning to make
his own way in the world. Crossing the streets is undoubtedly
a danger of the first magnitude in the life of today and yet

every child must learn at some time how to take care of himself on the city streets.

Another factor contributing to ego weakness is found when too much of ego development is turned toward countercathexsis, that is, behavior which runs exactly opposite to impulse. Every reaction formation involves a continuous outlay of energy, and where too much of the personality is involved with this form of disguise the drain on energy prevents a person from reacting spontaneously and effectively to situations that he confronts (59).

Changes in the Ego under Hypnosis

At this point, some comments on the influence on the ego in hypnosis will be made (24). Ordinarily hypnosis is thought of as robbing the individual of his ego strength as he voluntarily yields control of his behavior to the hypnotist. This is true so far as it goes, but it is a somewhat naïve and oversimplified conception of how hypnosis operates. Hypnosis is primarily a narrowing of the attention, and to the extent that attention is narrowed, the individual is prevented from responding to the wide range of stimuli to which he is ordinarily responsive. Hypnosis involves a certain loss of ego control. Under hypnosis there is a definite yielding of motor control. Through the blocking of inhibition, motor control is definitely weakened, so that under the hypnotist's suggestions an individual may react in ways which he would not permit himself to do in the waking state. He may be encouraged to put into action a conflict which hitherto he has been willing to express only verbally. One woman under hypnosis who previously could only talk about her dissatisfaction with her marriage took off her wedding ring and flung it across the room. It has been demonstrated that individuals can be brought to commit criminal acts under the influence of hypnotism. Hypnosis makes possible an acting out that ego control makes impossible in the normal state. Likewise under hypnosis there is a loss of emotional control so that an individual may give way to fits of weeping or of anger which he would not permit himself normally, and he may be more or less susceptible to the affects of anxiety, guilt, shame, and disgust.

Hypnosis also influences the thought process. Ordinarily an individual attempts to keep his thinking somewhat logical and avoids what he considers silly or absurd trains of thought. Under hypnosis, however, these controls are relaxed and an individual may give way to absurd fantasies including symbolism such as is found in dreams.

Under hypnosis there is a general weakening of defense mechanisms and impulses may express themselves more naturally, and there is less need to project, to rationalize, or to establish reaction formations against unacceptable impulses.

Pronounced diminution in self-awareness takes place under hypnosis. The individual may lose his sensitivity to touch, pleasure, pain, or temperature on the surface of the skin. The perception of equilibrium and motion is likewise altered, and the individual may become disoriented in space. There may be a loss of moorings. Perception of the body image may also become altered, distorted, or even lost. The individual may under suggestion adopt bizarre fantasies with regard to his body and the parts thereof. The individual may feel giddy, dizzy, and have fantasies of floating through space and the like.

Under hypnosis there may be a greater variability in ego functions than is noticed in normal life. Normally an individual maintains his ego functions with a high degree of consistency. One may be counted upon to do and say the same things in the same situations day after day. Under hypnosis, however, this consistency is altered and the ego becomes more variable, fluid, and receptible to suggestion.

Because the ego is under lessened control under hypnosis and because there are changes in self-awareness, it is possible to initiate changes in the ego functioning which may have therapeutic value. Contrary to popular opinion, being hypnotized does not necessarily mean permanent increase in ego weakness. Through hypnosis an individual may find release from constricting self-control which may enable him to work out a more effective integration of varying disparate parts of the ego structure.

Outcomes of Ego Strength and Weakness

Ego strength gives an individual a capacity to take the rebuffs of experience successfully without becoming submerged by them. As the ego develops, the individual is able to master new, dangerous, and painful experiences. Ego strength enables a person to deal successfully with calamity, loss, failure, physical incapacity, or even the death of some beloved one.

Ego strength also enables a person to master his affects of anxiety, guilt, shame, and disgust (59). This mastery may take two different courses. On the one hand, it gives a person courage to face his dangerous impulses of hate or of love. It permits him to dispel repressions and to express himself more freely and fully without arousing anxiety in so doing. But ego strength also in other circumstances may help an individual to reconstruct his repressions and place them on a more solid basis. By effecting a more thoroughgoing repression of dangerous impulses ego integration is helped, and this encourages still further ego strength. Probably the best adjustment involves both freeing the impulses on the one hand, so that they lose their dangerous qualities, and then, on the other hand, adopting their reasonable repression so that the individual can take an accepted place in society. Repressions on this basis are not forced and at war with tendencies within the self, but are more ego-syntonic.

Ego strength also enables an individual to become less dependent on the demands of other persons with whom he has affectional ties. It helps the young child free himself from dependence upon a parent and later in adolescence enables the growing boy or girl to form heterosexual ties and to feel less dependent on parental relationships.

On the other hand, ego weakness cancels these gains and makes the person more dependent. Where there is weakness in the ego structure there will be an impairment of mastery. In the young child this will show itself by less walking, talking, manipulation, and by general helplessness. In an adult this same breakdown of mastery will be known as a nervous breakdown in which the individual suddenly becomes helpless and is unable to carry on his tasks. When there is weakness in the ego structure the primary support for positive living is lost. A person with ego weakness becomes emotionally unstable and is subject to neurotic developments. When the ego is weak, instead of controlling his affects a person is controlled by them. Anxiety symptoms may develop, and as guilt rises there will be reactions of self-punishment and self-depreciation. Or the weak ego strives to gain control of its impulses by regression to forms of adjustment which were adequate at an earlier age.

The ego can be harmed by a too early restriction of emotional responses. Many parents in their zeal for perfection attempt to force children to adopt patterns of control too early, with the result that emotional development is squeezed out before it has had an opportunity to find adequate expression. Many parents harm the child by an overzealous attempt at cleanliness training in the early years. The child who becomes compulsive, rigid, and unresponsive as a result of these early efforts has really developed a brittle ego which is unable to meet shocks and deprivations to which it is not accustomed. Too much effort in self-control must be expended by the child who has been too rigidly trained in keeping down his repressions.

There are other dangers in premature ego development in the young infant that are not always recognized. Many overzealous parents will strive to make their child more competent and more self-dependent than he is ready for. Overzealous parents may undertake the task of training in cleanliness even in the first months of life and often children respond to these attempts. However, if the child adopts controls at too early an age, a stifling of personality is likely to develop and obsessional trends may appear somewhat later. For a rich and varied personality the infant needs freedom in emotional expression (77). The most spontaneous and expressive personalities are those that have been permitted to be natural and unrestrained in childhood. Melanie Klein (129) suggests that an attempt at too early ego development will interfere with a child's relations with reality and will stifle the development of fantasy. This will have repercussions on later intellectual development as well as cause distortions in the person's relations to the realities of life. Ribble (168) has made somewhat the same point in her emphasis on the necessity of fondling for adequate intellectual stimulation in the young infant.

8

THE RÔLE OF THE AFFECTS IN THE EGO

The Relation of the Ego to Anxiety

Anxiety, which mobilizes an individual's energy resources in anticipation of dangers, may be used by the ego as a warning that danger is imminent and that something must be done about it. Anxiety encourages the ego to react in anticipation of danger rather than to wait until the actual danger is imminent. Using anxiety as a signal, the ego anticipates the future and declares that even though the situation is not yet traumatic it might become so, and consequently takes up appropriate action to protect the self against the danger or to ward it off (59).

Anxiety is distinctly unpleasant and ordinarily the ego will do everything in its power to defend itself against anxiety, and yet anxiety is also endured because it serves as a warning. Anxiety is very much an affair of the ego (130). It is something the ego must learn to manage in some way either by tolerating it in small quantities or by warding it off.

In certain states of tension, however, the ego may call forth more anxiety than it can control. Frequently this happens when previous anxiety has not been wholly dissipated but remains in the form of residual tensions. In this case there is a trigger-like reaction, and with a supercharge of anxiety the result may be a panic reaction rather than reasonable and planned reaction to forestall anticipated danger. Normally anxiety is of great service to the ego in controlling the situation just ahead, as it constantly reveals itself; but when anxiety becomes overwhelming the reactions become diffuse and disorganized. Disintegration in itself is frightening and the very process of disorganization adds to the anxiety.

Disgust and shame serve a similar function in apprising the ego of anal and sexual stimulation for which it must be prepared. The ego uses disgust and shame as signals of dangers which enable it to defend itself against unacceptable anal and sexual impulses. Disgust and shame represent a collapse of the normal self-evaluation and immobilize the ego in helplessness until it recovers its aplomb and takes steps to renew its status and self-esteem (149).

Anxiety is closely related to success and failure, and both success and failure may arouse anxiety. It is clear why failure should arouse anxiety because it is a threat to self status, but it is not so clear why success may on occasion arouse anxiety. However, there are times when success itself is used as a defense against underlying weakness and the anxiety which it arouses. Success felt to be unmerited, that is, which deserves challenge and criticism, may bring on guilt. Also success may stimulate further ambition by raising the level of aspiration, which in turn may mobilize fears of further failure and punishment. Occasionally one finds a child in school who, although making an excellent record, is tortured by anxiety for fear that he may fail to live up to the reputation which he has gained. *Noblesse oblige* puts an added strain on what an individual expects from himself, and as expectation is raised the threat of failure is likewise increased. Sometimes the student in school who has had a long and unbroken record of successes feels strain because of the necessity to prevent a collapse in the record. The football team with a long string of unbroken victories feels a greater challenge with each game in order to maintain the unbroken record.

Anxiety plays an important rôle in ego development and organization (129). Any sensation, emotion, or mental function not under full ego control can seem intensely dangerous, and every person dreads experiences which he does not feel he can control. Much of the stimulus for ego growth arises from the desire to achieve the skills of mastery so that the ego can command its relations to objects and outer reality rather than be a defenseless prey to them. Anxiety is also a necessary stimulus for the development of fantasy and symbol-formation (127). Without anxiety there would be no attempt to anticipate future experiences. This anticipation of the future is the very essence of fantasy, as one tends to form images of what experience would be like. Anxiety, therefore, is basically at the root of thinking and is a necessary prerequisite for the development of language. Anxiety, however, which is to result in the development of fantasy and thinking should be mild and not overwhelming in intensity. Since fantasy and language are necessary for the most effective relations to reality and for sublimation, the highest development of human adjustment is rooted essentially in mild but basic anxiety. Looking at this matter from a slightly different point of view, ego development depends upon the ability to tolerate the inevitable anxiety which is aroused in response to mild frustrations and temporarily to postpone action in order to deliberate on the course of action to be pursued. If anxiety is aroused in the young child in too great amounts it cannot be tolerated, and consequently the response is of an emergency nature for the purpose of dissipating it or for defending the self against it. For the most advantageous ego development, anxiety should be stimulated only in an amount that the growing child can learn to tolerate.

The Place of the Ego in the Defense against Anxiety and Guilt

In the attempt to avoid anxiety the ego and the self also are involved in several ways. Hilgard (111) has said, "If one wants to understand a person's defenses against guilt we must know something of his images of himself." Symonds (197) has made it clear how guilt is introjected anxiety, that is, anxiety that is aroused when one is threatened by internalized figures —or standards—and when the impulses tend to go counter to these teachings. Hilgard goes a step further to suggest that guilt feelings involve self-reference that is missing from anxiety as such.

CONSTRICTION OF THE EGO

The principal method adopted to avoid anxiety is the constriction of the ego through excessive ego control and repression, a method that in a sense defeats its own ends. The ego may attempt to avoid anxiety by inhibiting perception— curiosity may be dulled and the individual may attempt to escape incoming impressions by foregoing reading, listening to the radio, or travel. By shutting off impressions from the outside, temptations can be avoided and anxiety can thereby be controlled. Anxiety may be kept under control by the general impoverishment of feeling, a state to be observed in obsessional neurosis.

Hilgard (111) reminds us that memories lost in amnesia usually have an intense self-reference, for they conceal experiences which are anxiety- or guilt-provoking. So much forgetting is purposeful forgetting, helping to prevent the recall of incidents that would arouse anxiety and cause distress.

Inhibition of Thought. Anxiety may also be avoided by the inhibition of thinking, and many persons have stifled their thinking processes in order to avoid the anxiety which would thereby be aroused. Many of these forms of inhibition of thinking have been described by Schmideberg (180). One may restrict his thinking for fear of criticism. Parents, for instance, may discourage curiosity and thinking in their children because they fear the questions which their children may ask or they do not wish to have to answer questions with regard to their own life which might be too revealing and damaging. There is a constant effort on the part of society to discourage critical scrutiny of forms of government and social institutions such as education, law enforcement, and the like. Children are taught too often to accept without challenge the present state of affairs, because sharp questioning might be embarrassing to those who would have to defend and justify their ways.

However, thinking may be inhibited because the asking of questions which are too revealing might also challenge the self. Ability to think means ability to stand assault to one's own self-esteem and to be able to tolerate the anxiety which might be aroused when one's self-esteem is threatened. Consequently most individuals fail to really question their own motives, preferring to let sleeping dogs lie rather than to arouse them to activity.

Some individuals are discouraged from trying to think because they thus are avoiding failure in thinking. Many persons would hesitate to attempt a crossword puzzle because they fear they might not be able to fill in all of the spaces. Another reason why thinking may be constrained is that in so doing one avoids facing one's real problems.

Much thinking is of a trivial nature, attacking problems without real import more as a gymnastic exercise and for the pleasure of intellectual mastery than of applying one's efforts to the working out of real individual or social problems. Thinking easily takes on an obsessional nature leading to all kinds of rituals and straight-jacketing. Some pedantic scholars will over-value names, dates, the use of words and the like. There is a tendency to let thinking take on stereotyped forms rather than to fit the exigencies of the problem situation at hand. There is often a need for symmetry, form, and regularity in thinking. Some persons show a stickiness of mind, becoming involved in minor and pedantic issues. There are others who show a fear of the unknown and a hesitation to explore beyond the familiar and the ordinary.

Schmideberg (180) points out how mental activities may serve as substitutes for physical ones, particularly when the physical is unacceptable and tabooed. "Thinking is in many respects a substitute for aggressive or sexual touching, for tasting and looking, for greediness and other forms of in-taking, for sexual activities and the excretion of bodily products." Where there is guilt over these bodily processes, the guilt may spread to thinking which has substituted for them and the result may be a distinct limitation in many forms of mental processes. In particular, guilt over sexual curiosity may spread to other types of thinking and cases have been reported in which children have been retarded in their work in school because their curiosity has been stifled by parents who have hushed them up when they asked embarrassing questions around the age of four (22).

Then there are instances of pseudo-stupidity or pseudo-imbecility in which a child, in order to avoid unpleasant consequences, has actually so inhibited his mental processes as to become dull and backward (128, 140). Stupidity may enable a child to maintain his relationships in the family. Stupidity which renders a child more or less helpless, by forcing the parents to wait upon him and give him devoted attention, may help him escape the anxiety of neglect. It may also be used to disguise aggression and thereby to escape retaliation. If a child can feign (unconsciously) stupidity he may escape punishment for acts of aggression which were also unconsciously motivated. A child may damage valuable household objects and then escape blame or punishment by maintaining the disguise of being stupid.

Excessive daydreaming may impair thinking, particularly if it is overindulged in. Fantasy as a substitute response to frustration serves to direct a person away from reality into the private world of his dreams. So instead of using his mental processes for a direct attack upon the problems which confront him he throws out his clutch and lets his engine idle without locomotion. The child who daydreams in the classroom escapes the necessity for giving attention to the classroom activities and fantasy thereby takes the place of purposeful thinking.

Frequently education itself crushes thinking. Sometimes the fault for this is the school's. Fearing too open scrutiny of real and vital social problems, a school may prefer to place the emphasis on memoriter learning or at least on accepting the teachings of the text without challenge. Often parents place the emphasis on knowledge rather than thinking and questioning, and prefer to measure their child's advance through school by the scores that he can make on tests of information and skill rather than upon his ability to ask questions and to challenge accepted opinions.

Schmideberg (180) points out that even scientific method may be used as a way of escaping thinking. Scientific method is upheld as representing the perfection of the thinking process. However, if a student becomes too obsessed with the canons of scientific method and follows accepted scientific procedure too slavishly he may fail to really inspect and think about the data with which he is working. Too much emphasis on the "design of experiment" may interfere with a more common-sense and realistic inspection of the data. Scientists in spite of their rigorous training often follow authority as passively as persons in any other field. It is interesting to note how the dictum of the "great authority" is listened to and how thinking is molded into the patterns that are laid down by those who occupy important "chairs" in important institutions. Scientists are often too much immersed in method and are unwilling to admit the real difficulties in thinking which are continually met as new problems create new conditions.

It has already been stated that anxiety may be avoided by experiencing less, by thinking less, and it is obvious that it may also be avoided by acting less. The control of impulses through inhibiting their expression in action is a well-known method of avoiding anxiety. Such examples as avoiding social intercourse, immersing oneself in work or study, or becoming immobilized through illness or accident readily come to mind. So with all three of the ego functions constricted, the result may be an inhibition and narrowing of learning capacity with an actual temporary decrease of the I.Q. Indeed whole developmental stages or parts of the ego may be repressed in the effort to avoid anxiety, leading to irreparable damage to development and adjustment.

THE COUNTERPHOBIC ATTITUDE

A second method by which anxiety may be avoided by the ego is the adoption of the "counterphobic attitude," a term proposed by Fenichel (57) to describe those forms of behavior in which anxiety is avoided by engaging strenuously in the very experiences which are feared. The person who fears high places will engage in mountain climbing in order continually to test and disprove his terror of heights. The man who fears for his possible lack of masculinity will attempt to demonstrate it by engaging in strenuous sports or by becoming the gallant lover. These compensatory methods are easily recognized by their exaggeration and inappropriateness. By the very strenuousness of the efforts to hide his fears, an individual reveals them.

REPETITION OF THE FEARED SITUATION

A third method of avoiding anxiety used by the ego is repetition of the feared situation. This point has been made in the discussion of reality testing. Briefly, as the individual takes an active rôle he is able to control the time and degree of excitation and hence is less defenseless than he would be when he is at the mercy of passive experiences. Children try out their anxieties in repetitious play (127). When fears are demonstrated to be groundless by facing them and finding that the situation is not as dangerous as was expected, the individual becomes more courageous and the repetition of the feared situation thereby becomes an effective method of reducing anxiety.

Normal individuals do not fear their impulses, for their strong egos can either gratify them without anxiety or can control them. So the capacity of the ego to master anxiety varies with ego strength. As the ego becomes more adequate both in terms of mastery and also capacity for repression, anxiety diminishes.

One further point should be made—namely, that the affects normally help to intensify the ego processes. Perception may be heightened under the stimulus of mild anxiety, for when the danger signal appears the ego becomes more alert and more sensitive to the spot from which the danger is likely to appear. Anxiety helps the ego to focus its attention on the critical spot and makes the attention more alert. It has already been pointed out that anxiety when not too strong and overwhelming is a very potent stimulus for thinking. And anxiety, as is well known, acts as a spur to activity, causing it to be more vigorous and to take place more rapidly. Indeed, the danger is that anxiety, if at all intense, will so stimulate immediate activity as to preclude the pause that is necessary for adequate consideration of the situation.

9

EGO, SUPEREGO, AND SELF-IDEALS

Freud's awkward term, the superego, which stands for those internalized expectations of parents and of the wider society, stands in close relation to the ego. Sherif and Cantril (191) have been unwilling to recognize the superego as being different in kind from other ego processes. It is believed that this leads to an unfortunate confusion and that actually Sherif and Cantril have included several different ego processes in their discussion. The superego, a product of introjection, represents an uncritical assimilation of the standards and expectations of parents and later of a wider society. The ego, on the other hand, should be thought of as the more critical assimilation of experiences with other people in the family and eventually in the wider society. Ego is based primarily on experience, on logical thinking and on the development of control. Superego is based on the promises of reward and threats of punishment and represents the uncritical assimilation of standards and expectations of behavior. For superego development there must always be some previous ego structure, otherwise the growing child would not be able to assimilate parental teachings and translate them into inner controls. Federn (52) has stated that the superego has no direct access to volition, that is, the superego responds only to what has been learned from others by voice, gesture, expression and the manipulation of others. But the self has access to bodily feelings and sensations and so is in contact with the responding side of the ego through the proprioceptive stimuli. Actually, however, superego development may proceed apace while the critical functions are slower in their development. The ego constructs the superego from its fantasies of good and bad parents. Actually any relation to an object leaves behind some alteration in the ego, either a change that is accepted uncritically or one that is assimilated on the basis of thoughtful judgment.

The ego stands between the demands of the basic drives on the one hand and the demands of the parents (who are representatives of the larger society) on the other. The ego has to respond both to outer reality as the child meets it and also to the superego which is its internalized interpretation of reality. It has been pointed out many times that the child's interpretation of parental demands and prohibitions becomes magnified so that the superego demands are often more extreme and violent than the actual demands of the parents in reality. The little child of two and three consequently must waver between objects in the real world and internalized fantasy objects. There should be a constant process of correction whereby parents clarify their expectations and thus bring the superego demands more closely into conformity with reality. Usually this means the reduction of superego demands rather than their intensification.

Because the superego represents the uncritical assimilation of parental expectations, it is inaccessible to judgment and intelligence. It is this inaccessibility to critical appraisal that makes the superego such a tyrant in many cases and forces the ego to be its slave. Actually logical judgment is often warped and complicated by guilt resulting from behavior which threatens the superego demands; that is, the superego may actually cause distortion and warping of thought processes.

Relations between the Ego and Superego

The relations between the ego and superego deserve extended discussion. In the normal individual they tend to be in agreement and the result is an absence of conflict and a harmonious working relationship, but due to the fact that the superego is more or less autonomous it can oppose and even exercise mastery over the ego. The superego may criticize the activities of the ego and actually exercise a censorship on impulses and thoughts. Because the superego exercises the functions of a censor it can make the ego miserable in its efforts to discharge impulses in a spontaneous, natural and healthy manner. The ego then must react to the superego in much the same way in which it has previously reacted to the parents, either by submitting or by rebelling, or by an alternation between these two methods. On the one hand, the ego may side with the individual's wishes and desires as against the wishes and desires of society and of its own inner representatives of society. This is usually recognized as naughtiness in children on the one hand and inner rebellion and guilt on the other. The ego may repress its superego and become criminal. Then the ego may, on the other hand, side with society and its inner representatives against its own wishes with resulting self-control and constriction of behavior. The most constructive relation, however, is that in which the ego mediates between the drives on the one hand and the superego on the other and effects a satisfactory working relationship between these two forces.

This conflict between the ego and the superego is intensified when the superego is hostile and restrictive and exorbitant in its demands. On the other hand, the conflict is lessened when the superego is mild, reasonable, and encouraging. The former condition develops when parents are demanding and punitive, whereas the latter condition is the result of parental relations that are reasonable, tolerant, and loving. Normally the superego and the ego need not be pitted against each other in conflict but they may work together in harmony, that is, the person may want to do the things that he has been told he should do. The ego and superego, however, may become warring factions when they work at cross purposes and the individual wants to do the things that he has been told he should not do and does not want to do the things he has been told he must do.

Normally society imposes restrictions which to some degree go contrary to normal impulses, so that there is always some ego-superego tension; but there are occasions, particularly when some crisis arises, when society may relax its strict moral standards and actually side with the basic impulses in man contrary to its own earlier restrictive teachings. For instance, war may help to integrate certain aspects of the ego and superego, as it permits—in fact, condones—aggressive acts toward the enemy which are ordinarily not permitted in peace time.

The conscience is the judgment of the ego in response to the demands or criticism of the superego. Where the two work in harmony one is ordinarily not aware of conscience. It becomes the "still small voice" when there is conflict between the two. The ego, for instance, is the part of the personality which confesses guilt (165). Penance and self-punishment are also ego functions and represent the attempt of the ego to reduce guilt feelings in response to demands by the superego. The ego may set up restitution tendencies as methods of combating the guilt which may be aroused when behavior does not live up to superego expectations. There may be an attempt to build, to construct, to make amends for earlier damage done either in fantasy or reality.

Like the parents, the superego can behave aggressively and

even cruelly toward the ego when the ego has failed to live up to superego expectations and can actually demand punishment. Masochism, the tendency to inflict pain on the self, is recognized as a sadistic drive of the superego against the ego which corresponds to the punishment which might be administered by parents. The person who becomes masochistic is recognized as one who has either abnormally strong and powerful needs, a weak ego, or a strong and demanding superego, or some combination of these. The individual who becomes strict with himself at the behest of superego demands has turned his aggression in upon himself and consequently is likely to be lenient and mild in his relations to others. This superego attack on the ego is felt as a loss of self-esteem and may result in feelings of inferiority and inadequacy. Alexander (3) has pointed out how sometimes an economic transaction seems to take place as though the ego in accepting self-punishment acts as if it had paid the penalty which the superego exacted and therefore is free to indulge itself in satisfying its cravings without further superego recrimination. Also by fulfilling superego demands the ego may experience an exhilaration ("what a good boy am I") which suspends or weakens the function of the ego in objectively judging reality. The overmoral individual shuts his eyes to many of the injustices about him, to which, if he were sensitive to them, he might react by making exceptions to the rules which he adamantly follows. The politician in Warren's *All the King's Men* was willing to resort to some rather questionable practices according to commonly accepted moral standards in order to advance social ends which he believed were fully justified on their own account (204).

Too early superego development along destructive lines may hinder ego development to the extent that a child puts extraordinary demands upon himself and turns aggression inward when impulses threaten to break through. The ego is thereby prevented from turning aggression outward and learning to adjust itself to the real world and developing skill and understanding.

A child may be helped to adapt to reality by being permitted to project his superego on to strong adults, that is, looking to his parents for support, control, and encouragement: "My father says it's wrong to gamble." Most children are helped in their ego development by associating with adults who are firm and decisive but not necessarily restrictive or punitive. With the encouragement and backing of the strong yet encouraging adult, the child is able to assimilate its superego demands and to integrate them with the growing ego.

Ego and the Self-Ideal

In latency and adolescence the ego and the superego may unite in pursuit of a common self-ideal. This ideal is patterned after strong adults whom the child admires and takes as his models, but basically the self-ideal is determined by the basic drives—to love and to be powerful. Schilder (177) points out that self-ideals are compromises between the demands for expression by the basic drives and the directing and controlling and repressing forces exerted by parents and other authoritative figures. In the well-integrated adult the self-ideal and the more restrictive superego are homogeneous and form a harmonious unity. What good parents hold as ideals for their children harmonize with the restrictive measures that they apply to them. More intelligent children, perhaps, can find their ideals in characters described in literature or even more abstract formulations of ideal expectations, but average children find their ideals in relatives or acquaintances in their actual experience. The growing child strives to mold its ego and to make it like the self-ideal. The self-ideal receives self-love similar to the love which was afforded it in reality by the parents in infancy. This love and appreciation is assimilated in the same way as other superego expectations and becomes a bulwark in helping an individual maintain self-esteem. With the assimilation of an effective self-ideal an individual has within himself an independent regulator of self-esteem. He becomes freed, to a degree, from evaluations made on him by society and can hold his self-respect with goals that may go contrary to the social group around him. Stability of character depends to a considerable extent on the acquisition of ideals which may be independent of immediate and temporary social expectations. Self-ideals develop most effectively when they have been fostered by strong father and mother models working in harmony which give the child support and self-respect. But even under the most ideal circumstances there is strife between various self-ideals for possession of the center of the personality. One may have to choose between moral ideals and ideals of success and achievement, or between ideals of helping oneself to advance and helping others.

Possibly the psychoanalysts have not sufficiently emphasized the importance of ideals in the mental economy. De Groot (43) is of the opinion that self-ideals are highly important factors in maintaining mental health and balance. They serve as internal regulators and help a person to maintain an even course in the force of the buffeting of circumstances. Self-ideals are the gyroscopes of personality. Self-ideals play an important rôle in maintaining the narcissistic position, that is, the self-evaluative tendencies of the self. But as de Groot points out, for mental health the self-ideal must not be too high and too demanding, nor too vague and shadowy, and yet high enough to give continuous support to self-respect. A man's self-ideals help him to be honest and faithful under temptation, to maintain a family in spite of centrifugal forces that tempt him away, to be regular and diligent in his work. The religious, ethical, and scientific achievements of mankind have been achieved through the assertive tendencies which have been spurred on by ideals, and it is the ideals of love that have helped to temper the destructive aggressiveness of mankind. It is the hope of the world that constructive altruistic self-ideals may be inculcated in every child through education beginning in the family and carried on through the school, press, and other means of communication.

IO

EGO BREAKDOWN AND DEPERSONALIZATION

So far this discussion of the ego has been concerned with ego growth and development. However, under adverse circumstances the ego can also go in the opposite direction and become less effective. This breakdown is actually a regressive phenomenon, and under conditions of extreme stress, ego functions may take on characteristics of an earlier period in development. Various phases of ego breakdown have been extensively discussed in the literature under the heading of depersonalization, and there is sizable literature on this topic. Depersonalization as a definite form of mental disturbance or an illness of a more enduring nature has been called true depersonalization; whereas when it is a phase of some other neurotic or psychotic disorder it is called temporary depersonalization. The signs of true depersonalization are recognized as symptoms, but when depersonalization is of a more temporary nature its manifestations are more in the nature of defenses. But it must not be thought that depersonalization is a state that is found only in well-defined and serious mental disorders. Mild forms of depersonalization are extremely common and few persons are able to operate at top levels of self-awareness and self-feeling. Mayer-Gross (142) points out a distinction between changes in the awareness and feelings with regard to the self and changes in the awareness and feelings with regard to the outside world, the latter of

which he calls "derealization." Galdston (90) likens depersonalization to a degradation in ego strength and intactness.

Nature of Ego Breakdown

Ego breakdown may exhibit itself in several ways. In the
first place, there may be a loss of inhibitory functions so that
impulses may break through into more open expression. For
instance, ego breakdown is frequently accompanied by intolerable tension and outbursts of uncontrolled anger or
weeping, in which the individual has apparently lost control
of his emotions.

Secondly, ego breakdown may show itself in instability in
relationships. Friendships may be more easily made and
broken and family ties which for years might have gone on
steadily may deteriorate. There may be difficulties in work
relations.

In the third place, ego breakdown may show itself in various
kinds of thought impairment. Thought may become confused
and disorganized. Concentration may be impossible and a boy
or girl at school may fall behind because of the impossibility
of concentrating on school activities. The capacity for discrimination may be impaired so that one is unable to choose
between the good and the bad or the acceptable and the unacceptable. There may be a loss of judgment so that a person
makes unwise decisions, bad investments, or embarks on enterprises unwisely. Thought may become confused and irrelevant
considerations may interfere with clear thinking, or there
may be an impairment of critical ability and self-evaluation.

Ego breakdown shows itself, in the fourth place, through
loss of self-respect and by a decrease in self-evaluation. A
person who becomes discredited in his own eyes, who lowers
his levels of aspiration, who complains of inability or ineffec-
tiveness is showing ego retrogression. This loss of self-respect
will reveal itself in loss of self-assurance, and a person who

has suffered loss or who has passed through some unnerving traumatic experience may embark on enterprises with less assurance or may even hesitate to undertake new things.

Another direction ego breakdown may take is in the development of mysticism and a falling back on the support of religion. Many persons who fail to meet the demands of complex modern living may "enter the church," and by absolving themselves of responsibility and giving up passively, find a haven in a more protected environment and a more dependent relationship.

LOSS OF INTEGRATIVE FUNCTION

A particularly important variety of ego breakdown is the loss of the integrative function of the ego, of which there are several types. In one well-known type, an individual may separate himself geographically from his fellows and go away to live by himself as a hermit. When an individual finds social living difficult and threatening he may be forced to withdraw and avoid the social contacts which stir up trouble within. A second type is the ego isolation of a more behavioristic nature, in which the individual, although continuing to live with others, becomes emotionally detached, fails to participate in the interests and activities of others, and becomes immersed in his own pursuits.

A particularly serious form of loss of ego integrative functioning is found in the many varieties of ego splitting where parts of the ego become detached from one another and go their separate ways. It is possible, for instance, for the ego to split into two or more of its original nuclei. The cases which were made famous by Morton Prince (163) are examples of the split personality. Robert Louis Stevenson has immortalized this split in the personality in his story of "Dr. Jekyll and Mr. Hyde." One does not have to go far afield to find such splits for they occur in lesser degree in everyday life.

The writer, for instance, has gathered fantasies of adolescent boys and girls in which quite regularly are described characters representing the good and bad side of their own impulses. Frequently these two opposing trends within will work themselves out in reality, and a boy or girl will alternately be amenable and diligent in school on some occasions and intractable and difficult on other occasions. In cases that approach the normal the individual is aware of these two opposing trends within and makes a determined, if feeble, attempt to harness them together or to find some working relationship between them. In more disturbed cases, however, the two parts do not recognize each other. Many individuals who develop delinquent trends represent just such a split in the personality. One part of themselves follows the demands of pleasure but another part responds to the demands of reality. Many delinquents alternate between giving free rein to their impulses and unconsciously seeking punishment in consequence of their guilt. Sometimes the split is of such a nature that the individual recognizes both forces at work but accepts one as being his own and projects the other onto the outer world or to some force foreign to himself. When a delinquent excuses himself by saying that he was forced to participate in a robbery unwillingly by members of his gang, the chances are that he is shifting the responsibility and failing to recognize the part that his own impulses had to play in the act. Another person may recognize his responsibility in the forbidden act but attribute it to a part of himself for which he does not feel responsibility: "It is not I who did it but a bad impulse within me." In still other cases, the mechanism of denial will operate so that the individual will deny the very personality trend which he is living out. A woman, for instance, may deny that she tends to depreciate and belittle men, whereas her every relation with a man is one in which she works unconsciously to cause him to fail in his endeavors.

Another type of loss of integrative function is to be found in those individuals who have an excessive development of "myness." In these individuals we see a striving for power and efforts to dominate others. These individuals have delusions of grandeur and of their own importance. They tend to bend everyone that crosses their path to meet their will. In thus failing to adjust to the needs and wishes of those around them they become increasingly isolated.

Still another more extreme type which has already been described consists of the dissociation of the self from its body. In such cases the individual has a sense of existing without a body and of feeling that his body is not a part of himself but in some way is foreign to him.

As the ego begins to lose its integrative functions, mechanisms appear in new and exaggerated forms in order to bulwark the split which has taken place and to prevent unwelcome impulses from breaking through into awareness. When the demands of unacceptable impulses become increasingly strong the split may deepen and widen and the defensive apparatus may increase in strength, leading eventually to those extreme forms of personality disorganization that are called psychotic.

It should be noted in passing that any process which damages the ego and renders it less effective at the same time hurts the self and valuation placed in the self. As the ego becomes less effective, narcissism is also hurt and the individual feels less adequate and there is loss of self-esteem.

Characteristic Expressions of Depersonalization

The foregoing signs of ego breakdown are also characteristic of depersonalization. However, there are a number of other signs that have been recognized as distinctively characteristic of depersonalization. In this state there are changes in the perception of space and time. Familiar landmarks appear strange to a person and he is unable to find his way around. He may also become disoriented with regard to time and be unable correctly to recognize events as pertaining to yesterday or tomorrow or to plan his activities with reference to a time schedule. There also may be disorganization in the perception of bodily conditions and change. An individual may have a feeling of unreality about parts of his body, as though a member did not belong to him and as though he had no concern with it.

In depersonalization there may also be disturbances of memory. There may be aphasia or a blotting out of portions of the memory of the past, or a memory may be badly distorted. Imagery may also be disturbed so that a person is unable to recall clearly images of persons or places or events. There may be a loss of feeling, particularly the feeling that accompanies action and that ordinarily gives tone to everyday experiences. An individual may plod through a day in a state of numbness, responding to each event in a dull, lifeless way, and he may actually deny the presence of desires which may seem to him at all wicked or dangerous. There may also be a lack of emotion. The individual may respond to situations ordinarily calling out emotion without characteristic love or hate, fear, anxiety or guilt.

Another sign of depersonalization is to be found in the person's attitude and bearing. The absence of feeling and emotion may show itself in impersonality, stiffness, formality and rigidity in social relations. The individual may become lifeless, a mere automaton going through the motions of the day's experiences without animation or vivacity. There may be an increase in passivity to be shown by retiring from social contacts, by failure to assert oneself, by loss of interest in undertakings, and by willingness to let other persons make decisions for him. In depersonalization there may be sensations of estrangement as though the individual was hiding something from himself. He may complain that the world in its ordinary aspects appears queer, dreamlike, and even frightening. In depersonalization there may be an increase in self-scrutiny and introspection and daydreaming. His friends may remark, "He's miles away," and he may sit for long periods wrapped in reverie.

Another sign of depersonalization is the tendency to identify oneself with another and live out one's aspirations and desires, hopes and fears through the experiences of another person. A girl who has been disappointed in a love affair or who has been severely repressed by her parents may seek to find her satisfactions through sharing in the experiences of her sister. She goes through life "as if" she were another person and derives all of her satisfactions from the conquests of her sibling. Cases have been reported where a younger child apparently has identified himself with an animal, perhaps a household pet, or even an imaginary cat or dog, thereby making it possible to experience in behavior or in fantasy certain wishes which are denied to him as a person.

A common sign of depersonalization is the increase in thinking and a tendency to indulge in abstractions. The scholar, whether he be philosopher, mathematician, or historian, may find the pursuit of his scholarly activities, with the high degree of abstractness that accompanies them, a method of removing him from his relations with other people. It has even been suggested that thinking may become eroticized, that is, that the pleasure that accompanies thinking may take on an erotic tinge. Akin to this concentration of activity on thinking is that of placing one's attention exclusively on objects (rather than persons) and becoming immersed in the details of machinery, laboratory experimentation, books, and the like.

Another sign of depersonalization is the conflict over the choice of fantasies, goals, or identifications and the doubts that arise from these conflicts. In particular, it has been noted that individuals in whom there is a clash between heterosexual and homosexual interests may show embarrassment and confusion over the choice of sex rôles. Perhaps the individual may have homosexual trends which are a source of embarrassment to him. Consequently, when he is tempted to show an interest in traits or behavior ordinarily thought of as feminine, he may repress them with signs of confusion. Obendorf (154) has described a syndrome which includes a sequence of these tendencies. He describes a man who, because of the threats from a father-figure, has turned in identification to a mother-figure and, following his mother, has adopted thought patterns involving a high degree of abstraction. However, thinking is considered by him to be a feminine activity and this is subsequently repressed because it betrays a homosexual attitude and conflicts with the male rôle which consciously he wishes to play. Perhaps this particular syndrome might be found rarely but at least it serves to illustrate some of the mechanisms which are to be found in depersonalization. In this instance, the outcome is a repression of thinking rather than its overdevelopment.

Finally, depersonalization may be expressed by a demoralization of the superego. Demoralization is an appropriate term to use in this connection because the individual loses his moral sensitivity and his moral standards, and engages in activities which hitherto would have been unacceptable to him from a moral point of view.

Factors Contributing to Ego Breakdown and Depersonalization

Psychoanalysts who have studied cases of depersonalization have found numerous factors which appear to have brought about this condition. These factors have been so numerous and diverse that superficially it would seem difficult to find any common principle running through them. However, when all of the data are assembled it would appear that de-personalization is one outcome of *parental rejection* which may express itself in many different forms. In some cases the individual had little or no breast feeding or the parent was careless and insensitive to the infant's needs. In some cases neglect seems to be the principal factor, while in others de-personalization seems to be a method which the individual has adopted to escape wrath, punishment, or the threats of punishment, criticism, or denunciation.

Depersonalization seems to be in general an outcome of uncertainties in human relationships. In most cases the indi-vidual has a not-loved feeling and frequently there is an over-developed need for admiration.

Schönberger (182), who observed the phenomenon of de-personalization in the upheavals of the war in Europe, believes that this condition is directly related to the disorganization of society. When there is a change in too many elements of the situation it will act as a trauma. Individuals need stable relationships. They need people on whom they can count who hold definite positions of authority. A person's house and furniture act as a stabilizing influence, and clothing helps to define the personality. Schönberger found that when a person was separated from those whom he knew and thrown in with strangers who were somewhat hostile to him, when his clothes and personal effects were taken away from him, and when he found himself in strange surroundings, symptoms of depersonalization would commonly arise. When a person's identifications are cut off and he becomes manipulated by alien forces, he finds it difficult to establish empathy with persons about him, and the absence of what is familiar neces-sitates a withdrawing into the self with the accompanying signs of depersonalization.

Depersonalization is also a response to punishment. It is as though the individual said to himself—"They may hurt my body, deprive me of my freedom, take away my possessions, but they cannot control my thoughts." So some individuals react to punishment by becoming stiff and lifeless, by devoting their attention to objects rather than persons, and thus making the self impervious to the dangers which threaten.

It is believed that depersonalization sometimes may have its origin in the Œdipus situation. The child who has a need to look on the one hand, or to exhibit himself, on the other, may respond to threats of parents by turning these tendencies in upon himself and indulge in introspection and self-scrutiny with a simultaneous reduction of tendencies to explore and respond to the world about him. It is possible that in some instances there is an identification with the harsh parent and the individual becomes severe and restrictive with himself as he introjects his parent's attitude toward him. In other cases, apparently the mechanism is to turn away from the harsh parent and identify the self with the other parent who shows more sympathy and understanding, but in such cases the individual may find it necessary to repress tendencies to identify himself with the parent of the opposite sex leading to more or less general inhibition of spontaneity. Sometimes depersonalization will exhibit itself through hyper-motility, restlessness and excitability, which apparently are compensations for and reaction formations against the lifelessness which is the first response to the threats which he has experienced.

From the foregoing conclusion that depersonalization is a result of failure to be loved, it follows that there may be a disintegration of personality when the person fails to love himself, that is, when he condemns as unreal all standards which he formerly held for himself. When a person is forsaken by his own superego, which dissolves under environmental pressures, then there may be more or less personality demoralization depending on whether there are compensatory supporting elements in the situation.

Galdston (90) suggests that some cases of depersonalization can be explained simply by the fact that the individual has never been taught how to integrate. In some families confusion and disorder are so paramount and so little attention is given to helping a child develop that the child adopts bizarre patterns of meeting the situations which he is forced to face. In other instances there are fixation points in development owing to special traumas that were experienced in passing from one developmental stage to another. Depersonalization in later life may represent a regression to these fixation points in development with all of the disorder and disorganization of personality which such regression entails. In all these instances the fundamental cause, so far as it is psychogenic in nature, can be summed up under the one term, "parental rejection."

Almost any difficult situation to which the person does not have the capacity for making adequate adjustment may initiate ego breakdown. Extreme deprivation such as loss of one's job, failure of love relationship, break up of marriage, and divorce are likely to cause personality disorganization. The ego may break down after too intense or too long continued stimulation, particularly where there is at the same time extreme frustration or monotony. The catastrophic effect of continued stress has been demonstrated many times over in the trials through which Europeans have gone during the war and postwar years. Bettelheim (21), reporting on prison camps, stated that it took from three to five years of uninterrupted punishment or pain to break down the desires of persons to remain the same, that is, to keep their nationality, their status, their occupation, and family connections. Some individuals of course succumb sooner than others to pressure. Where there has been a previous blocking of discharge through repression the individual is always more vulnerable to any threats because he is already under tension from within, and increased stimulation from without easily causes a rupture in the adjusting apparatus.

Separation from the group also tends to break through ego controls and tends to distort rational thinking. Many persons have difficulty maintaining their ego structure in new and unfamiliar surroundings, particularly where cultural standards differ from those to which they are accustomed. When a person migrates from the society in which he grew up, which may have been puritanical, to another society which is free and easy-going, it takes a very strong ego to resist modification under the relentless pressure of the new conditions. Equally disturbing is the collapse of established norms within a society. The collapse of society in Germany and Japan following their defeat in the World War has tended to disrupt the ego organization of citizens of these countries, which leads to the loosening of controls on the one hand and a general lowering of ego integration on the other.

It is well known that the ego becomes temporarily weakened under the influence of alcohol and drugs. Under the influence of alcohol resistances are lowered, impulses are expressed more freely, and there are various manifestations of ego breakdown. Naturally this is a temporary change and ego strength is restored when the influence of the drug wears off. However, whatever factors led to the need for lower ego resistance in the first place may repeat themselves so that under repeated stimulation there may be a gradual but permanent, ego deterioration. Studies [1] have indicated that oxygen deprivation will also result in the lowering of ego controls resulting in an exacerbation of unrestrained emotional expression.

[1] See R. A. McFarland, "The Psychological Effects of Oxygen Deprivation or Anoxemia on Human Behavior," *Archives of Psychology* No. 145, 1932. G. M. Smith, "The Effect of Prolonged Mild Anoxia on Sleepiness, Irritability, Boredom and Other Subjective Conditions," *Journal of General Psychology* 35: 239–250, 1946.

II

THE RÔLE OF THE EGO IN PATHOLOGICAL STATES

Rôle of the Ego in Neurosis

The nature of neuroses and psychoses cannot be fully understood without consideration of the rôle which the ego plays in these pathological states. A neurosis or a psychosis is a sign of ego weakness indicating that the ego is insufficient to gratify the basic needs of the individual and that it is forced to seek more primitive methods of meeting these needs. Writers like Federn (52), Galdston (90), Schilder (178), and Schönberger (182) emphasize that depersonalization or ego breakdown is a phenomenon in every neurosis. A neurosis strikes at the functioning of the ego and causes it to lose its effectiveness in perceiving, feeling, thinking, or acting; and depersonalization is a factor in every defense mechanism including, of course, regression. When anxiety threatens, as we have seen, the ego puts restrictions on its own organization and relapses to levels of functioning which characterize a more infantile condition. The egos of neurotics are restricted because of the necessity of devoting some of the available energy to maintaining defense mechanisms against unacceptable impulses. As an illustration, for instance, when the sexual or aggressive significance of any organ of the body increases, the ego function of that organ may be affected. For instance, if a child

163

finds that his eyes play an important rôle in his aggressive impulses (the "dirty" look) or his sexual longings (seeing what is forbidden), and his aggressive behavior or sexual curiosity has been punished, then he may repress the use of his eyes as a tool in daily living. For instance, cases have been reported in which children have failed to make progress in reading because they feared what they might see. So a kind of hysterical blindness prevented these children from reading, whereas their vision in every other respect was entirely normal (49).

A neurosis is a disease of the ego, a sign that the ego has been unsuccessful in effecting a synthesis of conflicting elements within. The neurotic symptoms are actually evidence that the ego is striving to effect such a synthesis (153). In many cases, neurosis indicates that the ego has been unsuccessful in meeting the demands simultaneously of an inexorable superego on the one hand and the persistent demands of the basic drives on the other. The ego's need to maintain its self-valuation comes into the picture. As the superego indicates that certain behavior tendencies are bad and socially unacceptable, the ego fears that if it were to gratify these bad impulses the result would be self-disgrace and a loss of self-esteem. Consequently, a neurosis is in part a conflict between the concept of the self as expressed in its wishes and the valuation of the self as expressed in its superego standards. A neurosis, then, is an adjustment that freezes the balance between the ego and the basic drives, but a balance that is on the whole unsatisfactory, for the reason that, the basic drives, on the one hand, are not wholly satisfied, and the self, on the other, is humiliated because of the inadequacy of the neurotic adjustment. The neurotic self is not a self to be proud of. Horney points out that one feature of a neurosis is a fall in the level of realistic self-esteem. Frequently a neurotic tries to bolster his evaluation of himself by unrealistic means—he takes pride in setting high and unrealistic goals—in being good, aggressive, unique, omnipotent, or omniscient. Neurotic trends tend to impair self-determination because the person is driven by forces over which he has lost control. Consequently a neurosis must be maintained by a constant output of energy.

The Neurotic Symptom

The neurotic symptom is a breaking through of repressed material into the ego organization, but in disguised form and in a way which does not wholly satisfy the needs which are striving for satisfaction. A symptom is a compromise adjustment and indicates that a forthright expression of a drive is too dangerous to be tolerated. It is a form of discharge without the complete consent of the ego. Perceiving, thinking, and acting, instead of enabling the individual to adjust to the world about him, have been partly loaned to the drives, on the one hand, and to the superego, on the other hand. Since the resulting behavior is a compromise in an attempt to satisfy both of these parties, it is not wholly satisfactory to either one, and the ego occupies a somewhat helpless and passive rôle between. A neurotic symptom is a form of reaction thrust upon the ego but without the ego's enthusiastic assent. Actually many neurotic symptoms are condemned by the ego; the ego is puzzled by them and is somewhat ashamed of them. Children, for instance, are ashamed of stuttering, enuresis, temper tantrums, thumb-sucking, and other similar neurotic manifestations. The symptom, therefore, is admitted by one part of the ego and yet is rejected by another part.

The phenomenon known as "secondary gain of illness" comes to the aid of the ego in its attempt to incorporate the neurotic symptom within the ego structure (86). For instance, the child who has a phobia of going to school finds that his parents are concerned and are attempting to help him make a good school adjustment. The secondary gain of illness here is the forcing of the parents to give time and attention to the child's problems. Although these same parents formerly were neglectful and rejecting, the child finds that his phobia incites them to give him their care and attention; and although having to miss school is intolerable, the excitement and sympathy which his difficulty arouses is a compensating factor. But, by and large, the symptom itself is a foreign body which perplexes and troubles, and in many instances the discomfort of a symptom which causes people to be annoyed or amused is sufficient to cause the ego to strive to find a better method of adjustment.

Specific Pathological States

HYSTERIA

In hysteria, which ranks as the neurosis involving the least amount of regression, the ego retains the highest degree of strength (3). In hysteria repressions are strong and the hysterical symptom becomes a substitute for the tendency which is repressed. In hysteria, memory becomes faulty and unreliable, particularly as it concerns the drive which is repressed. In hysteria the symptom breaks through in distinct opposition to the ego and without the ego's coöperation. The symptom becomes a substitute for more direct action. Some perception or motor response which has become unacceptable is interfered with, and hence ego control over it is damaged and the hysterical symptom which takes the place of the perception or motor response apparently acts without the complete assent of the ego. Stuttering becomes a substitute for aggressive speech. Nail-biting may become a substitute for, and protest against, the use of the hands for hostile aggression or masturbation. Because the repression is so complete, the ego does not have control over the symptom, which seems to be an involuntary reaction. Actually, however, the shift from an unacceptable impulse to some physical disorder is a relief, but not a wholly satisfactory relief. Because of the strength of the repression, the ego is spared the painful experience of perceiving that which has been criticized by the superego and hence escapes guilt. In hysteria the ego is not aware of the impulse of which the hysterical symptom is a substitute.

PHOBIA

In a phobia the ego uses a somewhat different method of avoiding recognition of unacceptable impulses by referring them to some outside danger. However, in making this adjustment the ego gives up some of its freedom and mobility. By having to avoid the dangerous situations and by having to widen the circle of what is considered dangerous in order to maintain the repression of awareness of the dangerous inner impulses, the ego has definitely limited certain of its areas of expression. If the phobia is slight this restriction can be tolerated, but if too large an area of life is thus avoided, then the ego may have to take steps to find a better method of adjustment.

COMPULSIVE NEUROSIS

In the compulsion the ego is relatively strong, but in a somewhat different way than in hysteria. In a compulsion the ego attempts to effect a compromise between the superego and the impulses which are to be warded off. The compulsive act gives partial expression to the impulse, but in a disguised fashion and in a manner which apparently prevents the impulse from gaining wholly satisfying expression. Compulsions represent not only an attempt to obey the superego but also to resist it in order to ward off guilt. If a mother were forced to think again and again how horrible it would be if her son were to experience an automobile accident going to or coming from school, this compulsive thought would be a protest against the possibility, and yet the very compulsiveness of it would indicate that its possibility was harbored in fantasy. Much compulsive thinking represents a preparation for and a protest against acts which are never performed. By the very protest against these acts, the superego sway over them is recognized, but the basic demands as well as the threat of loss of love or of punishment from the superego (59) bring the obsessional thought up again and again into consciousness. So in compulsion the ego vacillates between desire and repression. Compulsive behavior indicates a certain degree of ego immaturity. Problems are never really squarely faced, and the individual vacillates between working out a solution and meeting the demands of the superego. Compulsive trends are frequently the result of early and rigid development of the ego at the expense of emotional expression, which is thereby stifled.

SCHIZOPHRENIA

In psychotic states the ego breakdown has reached an advanced stage. Snygg and Combs (192, p. 165) attempt to explain psychosis in terms of the self, affirming that the difference between a psychosis and a neurosis lies in the degree and extent of the threat to the organization of the phenomenal self. How much the picture of the self enters into the determination of psychosis is open to conjecture, but certainly to the observer there is deterioration of ego functions as well as of the individual's self-concept. Schizophrenia is the name given to a variety of expressions of ego breakdown and disorganization. In schizophrenia there is a collapse of reality testing. On the one hand there is withdrawal from reality, and on the other thinking becomes confused, trivial, and disorganized. There is a tendency to return to the state before the ego was established and to become helpless and non-adjustive. Galdston (90) states that many of the schizophrenic's symptoms show signs of depersonalization. The schizophrenic, for instance, may find pleasure in mental processes for their own sake. The depersonalized person maintains that in reality nothing has changed, although he may say that things seem different; but the schizophrenic is persuaded that the world is really different—remote, difficult to understand, and impossible to operate in.

MANIC-DEPRESSIVE STATES

In depression the ego shows considerable weakness. It yields to the demands of the superego, and the fury with which the ego formerly attacked other objects is now turned against the self. Instead of attempting to ward off guilt, guilt is accepted and the full force of the aggressive tendencies is turned inward. However, even in depression the ego is acting to effect a restitution of self-esteem. In melancholia, for instance, there is evidence of strong identification with the lost object or person, and the turning in of aggression on the self is in part an attempt to recover the lost object by incorporating it into the self. In melancholia, for example, one may strive to carry out the wishes of the lost person or to make a beginning of carrying on in his place and of achieving his ideals.

In manic states the ego also shows its weakness, but in a different way. In manic states inhibitions are suspended and impulses are given free rein. Also there is an overpowering of the superego as the individual performs acts which indicate the loosening of old superego standards. In manic states there is a loss of ego control. However, the superego may eventually assert itself so that guilt will cause a swing back to the depressive condition when aggression again will be turned inward.

PERVERSIONS

Freud has analyzed perversion in terms of a splitting of the ego. According to him, the perverse sexual act is acceptable to the ego because other impulses are repressed and denied reality. In hysteria the sexual impulse is repressed and the hysterical symptom takes its place as a partially acceptable substitute, but in perversion some sexual practice remains acceptable because some other idea has been denied.

TICS

Tics and other forms of involuntary motor performance must again be recognized as a split in ego organization. Some behavior, continuing to operate without voluntary control, may express significant symbolism in an act which, if its symbolic significance were fully recognized, would be unacceptable. For instance, clearing of the throat may be a remnant of a desire to utter some aggressive word which is repressed but still is permitted this remnant of a response.

12

THE PLACE OF THE EGO AND THE SELF IN PSYCHOTHERAPY

In cases where ego development has been retarded or distorted and there are cracks or weaknesses in the ego structure it may be necessary to give the child, the adolescent, or the adult help in strengthening his ego functioning. This process of bolstering the ego in contrast to the natural process of ego development is known as *psychotherapy*. Freud, who has set the pattern for many of our present psychotherapeutic practices, did not recognize the importance of the ego until late in his career. His first efforts at curing emotionally sick people was directed toward the reduction of symptoms. Later, however, as his perspective broadened, he saw that in order to help a person who is mentally sick it is necessary to treat him as a whole personality rather than in terms of separate bits of behavior.

Psychotherapy as Ego Development and Strengthening

The task of psychotherapy is to provide the best possible conditions for ego functioning (41). Usually the hindrances are to be found not only in the external environment but also in certain blocks and conflicts within the individual. Just as ego development is a process of becoming less dependent on others and becoming more self-directing and dependent on one's self, so psychotherapy, too, has these as its goals, and it attempts to help an individual pick up where his development stopped in early life and continue with the maturing process. The ego resists change because any change becomes a threat to its stability and its integration. Therefore a considerable part of the task of psychotherapy is to provide sufficient security so that some of the immature elements of the ego organization of an individual will be relinquished in favor of more effective and mature ego controls. With a strengthened ego an individual should be better able to stand up under strain and to avoid neurotic methods of meeting difficulties in the future.

It is an interesting point that psychotherapy itself must work through the aid of whatever ego strength the person has already acquired. Without some ego structure there would be very little with which to work and one would have to start a process of psychotherapy on a very low level of functioning. To the extent that a person has certain elements of ego strength—the capacity for self-control, some adeptness at reality testing, and a certain degree of ego integration—there is a foundation on which to build.

In psychotherapy ego strength is instilled at all stages of the process by identification with the therapist, who in his own life exemplifies good ego functioning (208). The patient is helped to attain ego strength in large measure by the relationship which is built up between him and the therapist. Self-esteem may be reinforced on a superficial level through the warmth and friendliness of the therapist, who thereby encourages self-independence; and an increase in self-esteem goes a long way toward helping a person attain feelings of adequacy and better adjustments. Since the ego of the neurotic has remained immature, frequently because of insecurities in the early years of life, it is necessary to provide such security in the relationship between therapist and client which will enable ego growth to continue from points where it stopped developing.

To the extent that an individual is aided in recognizing and accepting his feelings and releasing his tensions his ego becomes stronger and is better able to deal on a more rational and constructive basis with the daily situations which he has to meet. Both Rogers (173) and Snygg and Combs (192) emphasize their belief that a reorganization of the self will result in a change in behavior, and changes in behavior are outcomes of changes in the concept of the self. Aidman (2) and Sheerer (188) have demonstrated that as feelings toward the self change in psychotherapy there is a corresponding change in feeling toward others. Rogers and Raimy (166) present evidence to demonstrate that strengthening one's acceptance of himself results in more confident, outgoing action.

Psychotherapy and the Superego

One important goal of psychotherapy is to effect changes in the superego. The individual with neurotic adjustments needs to be helped to become more clearly aware of his superego tendencies and perhaps to loosen the hold the superego has on him. Psychopathic and psychotic individuals, on the other hand, whose ego functioning is very immature, may need superego development and strengthening so that drives can be repressed. For the neurotic, reduction of the strength of the superego does not necessarily mean that superego standards and demands should be diminished, but that they should operate in a less tyrannical fashion. The individual needs to acquire flexibility with regard to his superego standards, and the feeling that he deserves punishment when he does not come up to his standards should be reduced. The healthy individual maintains standards and controls of behavior but feels less guilt and self-abnegation when he does not totally live up to his own self-expectations. With a less tyrannical superego, an individual is better able to reconcile his superego demands with the demands of reality (129).

Psychotherapy and Ego Integration

The principal task in all forms of psychotherapy is to incorporate into the ego structure unconscious contents that have been withheld and which are consequently unacceptable and have not been integrated into the total ego structure (59). Rogers (173) has said, "It could appear that when all of the ways in which the individual perceives himself—all perceptions of the qualities, abilities, impulses, and attitudes of the person, and all perceptions of himself in relation to others— are accepted into the organized conscious concept of the self, then this achievement is accompanied by feelings of comfort and freedom from tension which are experienced as psychological adjustment." But it is probable that this relief and freedom from tension are not accomplished until the person is helped to reorganize his concept of himself.

Alexander (6) asserts bluntly that repression is undesirable in a mature adult. According to this point of view the healthy ego is in touch with all of the forces in the personality and permits expression, where possible through adjudication of differences and compromise, of all needs, desires, and interests as well as those trends which represent the controlling and directing forces of society.

Psychotherapy may be thought of as a process of education by which the ego is helped to become aware of and to tolerate and control impulses and drives which the superego rejects as bad or infamous, particularly those which originated in infancy and persist only as unconscious fantasy. To be more specific, as an example, it is not uncommon for neurotic individuals to express in their dreams distinct death wishes toward individuals with whom they are closely associated as, for instance, members of the family. Some psychotherapists regard these death wishes as remnants of attitudes held in early life and long since disregarded and repressed in favor of more recently acquired and socially accepted attitudes which constitute the superego.

The task of psychotherapy is to help individuals acknowledge these deeper feelings and impulses, to recognize their fantastic nature, to see on what a thin foundation they were based, and how utterly unrealistic they are at the present time. As these unconscious impulses are thus brought to light their tenuousness helps them to dissolve into thin air and their grip on the personality is lessened.

However, these unconscious elements were originally made unconscious because such thoughts and impulses were not tolerated by parents and teachers in earlier years, and continued recognition of them would be anxiety-provoking. In order to defend the ego against anxiety, resistances are built up against the recognition of these unconscious impulses. The task of therapy is principally that of breaking through these resistances which serve as a barrier to the conscious recognition of the impulses which are thus kept out of conscious awareness. However, even after the resistances are broken through and the ego is helped to become conscious of inner trends of which it was not aware, there is still the necessity for a process of reëducation in which the ego is encouraged to give up the repressions which it has so long harbored (77). Hilgard (111) suggests the desirability of defeating the mechanisms which serve the purpose of resistance either by simply bringing them to consciousness so that the person may decide whether or not to use them, or by seeking out the underlying motive for them so that the person may find out for himself whether they are necessary. But Buchenholz and Frank (29), who saw persons who were disorganized from war experiences in World War II, were satisfied to be able so to strengthen the ego that old mechanisms could function again as they had more or less successfully functioned before.

Psychotherapy and Threats to the Ego

Rogers and his followers (102) discuss resistance under the heading of threat. They believe that it is necessary to shield the client from threat if therapy is to proceed apace. For threat forces a person to defend himself, and under defense a person clings to his self-concept, and the aim of therapy is to help a person to change his self-concept in favor of a more adequate one. A person under threat with perceptions narrowed and many of his tendencies repressed is simply unable to conceive of himself in a different way—he is not in contact with his unconscious processes—and he is unable to perceive that any other possibility exists in his relationship to the world about him. Until the fairy godmother arrived Cinderella could not conceive of herself as being anything but an ugly drudge. But as, through counseling, a person achieves a wider perspective of himself and the world about, then it becomes impossible for him to maintain his former concept of himself. As Cinderella was helped to see herself as having the capacity to be charming and as the possibilities of her attending the ball were revealed, it was no longer tolerable for her to conceive of herself as the drudge sitting in the ashes.

It is to decrease the possibility of threat that emphasis has been placed on the acceptingness and permissiveness of the counselor. This means that the therapist must avoid any trace of threat in the form of criticism, belittlement, or disagreement with not only the client's behavior but also his attitudes and thoughts. It is a well-known principle of psychotherapy that the therapist must be convincingly accepting of the client in every respect. A critical, belittling, or hostile attitude on the part of the therapist will defeat his purposes from the outset. Not only must the therapist be accepting but he must also be permissive, which means that he must not attempt to steer or guide the client into ways that he (the therapist) believes would be desirable. Rather, he should wait until the client has accumulated sufficient ego strength so that he himself can control and guide his own behavior. In practically every case, particularly of neurosis, the fault lies not in the client's ignorance of the conditions of happiness or what society expects of him but in the failure of his ego to guide and control behavior along desirable lines.

The counselor rigidly adheres to the rule that he should never anticipate a feeling or attitude which has not been more or less openly expressed by the client. It is believed that by following this rule there is a decrease in defensiveness in the client. But there is always a possibility that threat will again and again be encountered as deep-lying values are exposed, so that there is constant need for watchfulness against the possibility of exposing the client to threat.

Coöperation of the Ego in Psychotherapy

Psychotherapy involves a splitting of the ego whereby a reasonable side which is responsive to reality works in coöperation with the therapist against the defensive side which is attempting to keep unconscious elements from exposure to the light of awareness (195). Unless there is a portion of the ego which can work coöperatively in the interests of a more thoroughgoing integration, psychotherapy is impossible.

There are two types of mental disorder for which psychotherapy is extremely difficult or impossible. One consists of those highly narcissistic individuals who have difficulty in establishing a trusting relationship with any other person. If there is no part of the ego which can work with the therapist, the therapist has no handle with which to begin his work. The other group of individuals are those with psychoses who have so isolated themselves and withdrawn from reality that they have no part of the ego which is accessible and which can coöperate in regaining mental health. The psychiatrist who wishes to work with psychotic patients on a therapeutic basis must be content to work with whatever small fraction of the rational ego is left with which he can get into contact (194) .

Methods for Achieving Changed Perceptions of the Self

In psychotherapy the client is called to coöperate with the therapist against other elements in the ego which are working at cross purposes with the rational. There must always be a change in the ego if it is to remain and deal with painful impulses. Combs (38), with his phenomenological bias, states the task of therapy as that of creating a situation in which change of perception (of the self) is formulated and encouraged. Rogers (172), in his client-centered therapy, watches patiently while the client, through his own efforts but aided by the tolerance and acceptance of the therapist, works out a new perception of himself and gradually finds tolerance for inner forces which enables him to reorganize his attitude toward himself and become more self-directing.

Combs (37) indicates that when the counselor openly recognizes and accepts the feelings expressed by the client he is doing more than help him to accept these feelings. As the client is helped to focus his attention on the meaning that experiences have for him, he is clarifying his perception and concept of himself and his relationship to the people and events around him. As in any problem situation when the issues are sharpened and narrowed, vague uncertainties evaporate and one can focus his attention on the problems at hand. And with this clarification it is possible for a person to shift his concept of himself, to change the gestalt, to approach the world and his relationship to it with a fresh point of view, and hence to achieve better adjustment.

Moreno attempts to help a person gain this self-insight more directly by the psychodrama than by indirect methods. Toeman (200) explains how, by the use of an auxiliary ego in which both the subject and the auxiliary ego participate or by the use of a "mirror" technique in which the subject remains in the audience, the patient is helped to gain some realization of his own behavior.

Many psychoanalysts believe that except in the mildest cases of ego disturbance the nondirective method would be ineffective. The psychoanalyst works through interpretation, principally the interpretation of the patient's resistances, by pointing out to the patient how, through his rationalization, his projections and other forms of evasion, or through his acting out, he is avoiding facing unpalatable truths about himself. As the patient is able to accept these interpretations and understand the defensive nature of his behavior it becomes increasingly possible for him to face and accept those actions, feelings, and defenses which he was formerly unable to accept.

It is believed that this interpretation is most effective when it concerns the attitudes which the client is expressing in the therapeutic sessions themselves and particularly those which are directed toward the therapist. A little child may show outright hostility toward the case worker who is attempting to help him. It is a simple matter for the therapist to point out to the child his feelings, and insofar as the therapist accepts these feelings without punishing or criticizing, the child is helped to accept his feelings himself.

Raimy (166, 167), through his analysis of cases treated by Roger's methods of nondirective therapy, demonstrates that one outcome of this type of psychotherapy is an increase in self-approval and self-acceptance, and he believes that these changes are signs of fundamental changes taking place in the personality. Having accepted these feelings in the therapeutic situation, it becomes easier for the child to accept them in other situations, and the very acceptance of them reduces the necessity to express them.

As an individual is helped to recognize and accept forbidden feelings and impulses they become less threatening and dangerous. Superego standards with regard to them may not change, but the ego becomes less afraid of these superego demands. To put the matter more simply, a child may still believe that it is wrong to strike or harm another person but he is better able to accept his feelings of anger against others, and the very acceptance of these feelings reduces their strength. However, the exposure of unconscious feelings always arouses anxiety, and anxiety is never easy to bear. Consequently, this process of pointing out and tolerating the individual's unacceptable impulses by the therapist must be repeated over and over again as the client continues to express them. This is known as the process of "working through." It is this therapeutic process which helps the ego to bear increasing tensions.

If the pain of the anxiety which exposure of unacceptable parts of the self might arouse is too intolerable, the ego may refuse to use the worker and break off treatment. This outcome is seen in many instances when parents bring their children to the clinic for help with regard to their handling, and the worker, in talking to the mother, helps her see that the children's problems are related to her own problems. As this insight breaks through, so much guilt may be aroused which becomes so intolerable that the mother is unable to permit the child to come for treatment and breaks off the process. Or in other cases where the mother is willing to let the child come for treatment, she is unwilling to explore her own relationships to the child's problem because of the guilt which it arouses.

Importance of Diagnosis as a Prerequisite for Psychotherapy

No process of psychotherapy should be undertaken without a preliminary diagnosis of the nature of the difficulty. In some cases the individual's problems are the result of some immediate traumatic experience which has temporarily impaired the ego's functional efficiency. In such cases a type of supportive therapy is called for which will give the person being treated support until he is able to face his situation and make adequate adjustment to it (7). However, some clients may attempt to interpret their own problems as though they represented different kinds of a temporary impairment because of their resistance to recognizing its neurotic background. It is true that during the war many men with otherwise stable personalities were temporarily unnerved and disorganized by severe traumatic experiences. Ordinarily, however, when an individual is broken by some overwhelming experience one should suspect a weakness in the character structure which has a longer history and which must be taken into account in repairing the damage.

Variation in Psychotherapy for Different Types of Mental Disorder

One should recognize that the therapeutic task varies according to the type of mental disorder. In hysteria there is already a healthy ego structure which can be used by the therapist to work with him in breaking through the defenses against unconscious attitudes and feelings. In the compulsion neuroses on the other hand, a larger portion of the ego sides with the resistances and the resistances are more difficult to break through. In particular, the compulsive neurotic may use the mechanism of isolation in which a portion of his personality is walled off through lack of feeling and it becomes very difficult to integrate this isolated part of the ego into that portion of the ego which feels. For instance, some compulsives have so intellectualized their problems that although they can discuss them apparently with great rationality, no progress is made in breaking through to the wishes and impulses beneath because their intellectual approach is so devoid of feeling. When one passes over into the psychotic states the withdrawal from reality is even more pronounced and the therapist has still less with which to work in helping the individual to make contacts and to break through the wall which separates his impulsive nature from the more reasonable parts of the self.

13

EDUCATION FOR EGO AND SELF DEVELOPMENT

The ego, as the term is used here, refers to that phase of personality which mediates rationally and constructively between the inner needs of the organism and the outer environment. The ego is the rational side of man's personality in contradistinction to the more primitive basic drives and emotions. Although each individual reacts to the situations which he confronts according to his inner needs and drives, and although anxiety is aroused in situations where he feels threatened and much of behavior consists of various mechanisms as defense against anxiety, man also has rational capacities which enable him to anticipate frustration and to work out solutions to the situations which block him. It is true that most persons meet their problems impulsively and emotionally instead of rationally and constructively, but each individual has capacities within him which can be developed to be used in meeting more effectively the problems and frustrations which arise in daily living. The basic tendencies of aggression and the so-called mechanisms of defense against anxiety seem to operate naturally and without tutoring, but the ego or rational side of man requires cultivation and exercise.

The development of the ego may be considered the main task of education. Education should be concerned with helping individuals make better adjustments to their physical and social surroundings. Education should be concerned with more effective perceiving, more effective thinking, and more effective acting. Too often schools forget that their task is helping boys and girls grow up to be more efficient men and women. They become so immersed in the details of the process of growth that they forget the larger aims. Schools may become concerned with the development of such isolated skills as reading, writing, and arithmetic without providing that these skills be directed toward developing increased competence in the affairs of life. But modern education recognizes that these skills have a functional value and makes provision for the development of them in the situations in which they are to be used. The process of growth is one of changing from dependence on others to dependence on one's own efforts, decisions, and controls.

Respect for the Ego of the Growing Child

Respect for the ego of the child at every stage of growth is highly important. It is easy to forget that even the very young child is striving to attain competence and that his efforts to attain mastery should be respected from the beginning. The ego grows by exercise, and a child should be provided with the opportunity of exercising all of his ego functions. He should be encouraged to attend to objects about him, to become curious about the relations of things and of persons, to think about the issues that confront him in daily living, to consider alternate plans, to anticipate the outcomes of various actions, and to learn to make rational decisions concerning them. The child should be given an opportunity to experiment and explore, rather than be restrained from these activities.

Parents should recognize that the ego grows gradually and

slowly. Ego functions follow a natural sequence in development and it is unwise to attempt to force them ahead of the schedule which nature has provided. There is never reason to regret waiting until a later time to encourage a child to undertake new forms of learning, but this should not be interpreted to mean that a child should be kept dependent. But what the child might attempt to do today he can also do equally well, if not better, next week or next year.

Freedom as a Necessary Condition for Ego Development

Parents and teachers should give a child as much freedom for choice, decision and learning by experience as he can stand. Here there must be moderation between two extremes. On the one hand, there is the attempt to delay the passage of each stage of a child's development by the mother who dreads a child's growing up and wants to keep him dependent as long as possible. Such a mother will wean a child late, will dread the time when he leaves home for school, and later in adolescence will resist every effort of the child to become independent and make decisions of his own. The other extreme is found in those parents who shove the child ahead at each stage of development. These parents seem to be threatened by a fear that the child will not grow up and are constantly urging the child to take more initiative and more responsibility than he is ready for. Children who are overprotected will sometimes attempt to do things on their own initiative in crude and unreasonable ways. On the other hand, children who are thrust ahead before they are ready will seem to lean back and require more than ordinary care and urging. It is believed today that the best results are achieved when more rather than less care and nurturing are given at each stage. Today confidence and security are emphasized in education, for it is believed that children who feel the most secure are also the ones who will dare to experiment and explore the most.

The harm that comes to growth from ridicule and criticism probably needs no emphasis, and yet in countless instances parents and teachers express their hostility to children by these methods and thereby frighten or shame children from exploring or thinking or acting.

Encouraging Children in Active Participation

Children should be encouraged to be active and participants in enterprises rather than to be passive and recipients. It is too easy in many cases for parents to assume the responsibility and do for the child what he could do for himself (because it can be done more efficiently) than to give the child the opportunity of trying out things for himself. Some parents will do their child's homework in order to ensure that it is well done, thereby depriving the child of experiences that will contribute to his learning and development. Families and schools should include children in a discussion of difficult problems which have to be faced and in the making of plans. Children will learn best when they are given an opportunity to participate in the common activities of the group.

Authoritarianism versus Democracy in Ego Development

The place of authority and dominance in ego growth is often misunderstood. To be sure, a certain amount of dominance from one's elders is necessary for a child's acculturization. However, it is easy to carry the practice of domination too far. Autocracy in any human relation discourages self-direction and self-control and these are the aims of ego building. Much more is to be expected for ego development from a democratic organization of the social group in which respect is felt by all the members for each other, in which freedom of thinking and action is given to all and in which there is mutual assistance and participation in family activities (176). Children will learn more in the process of fitting into social expectations through the process of sharing than through dominance from above. However, in those instances in which a child has lived in an authoritarian atmosphere, liberation from control may place too heavy a burden on the immature ego. The shift from authoritarian controls to more democratic forms of control must proceed gradually and cautiously to make sure that the immature egos are not given more responsibility than they can manage.

Fries (89) has pointed out a number of factors to be considered in selecting experiences for ego building. She is particularly sensitive to congenital and constitutional differences in personality from her studies of new-born infants and warns on the one hand against forcing and inconsistency in the handling of the slow and lethargic child, and on the other hand points out the necessity for restraint and correction of the overactive child. In planning ego building experiences, physical status must be considered as well as mental capacity. Gifted children present peculiar problems in ego development because of the disparity between their ability and their emotional immaturity. Gifted children frequently can solve problems on an intellectual basis before they are emotionally and physically ready to meet new situations. Other factors to be taken into account are the age of the child and special experiences such as travel, being under the guidance of a nurse, or a severe illness. Fries also suggests that one must look ahead to the results intended as a result of ego building experiences, and they must be planned to fit the child into the culture in which he will probably live as an adult. Of special significance is the adult's attitude toward the child. Every child deserves being under the care of an emotionally mature adult who will not respond by envy, on the one hand, or disappointment, on the other, at the progress the child makes in his development.

Aids to the Development of Thinking

Many of the points already made apply with particular force in encouraging the development of thinking (198). If children are to grow in their ability to approach situations thoughtfully they must be given freedom to think for themselves. It is so easy to think for a child because his attempts to think are so clumsy and ineffective; but learning takes place only through exercise, and if a child is to mature in his ability to think he must be given the opportunity of practising thinking.

Children will learn a lot by being permitted to participate in the thinking activities of others. Since thinking is something that does not take place openly where it can be seen or heard, it is especially important for parents to carry on their thinking in ways in which a child can participate. A child will be helped greatly in his growth in thinking if he can witness or participate in free discussion, and the parents are wise if they will engage in lively discussion and encourage the children to join in with them.

Children should be praised for their attempts to think rather than be belittled or criticized because their efforts are childish and ineffective. Children around the age of four, perhaps, do not need to be encouraged to ask questions, but at least they should not be discouraged from asking them. Children's questions should be considered seriously and reasonable answers should be given. Naturally a parent cannot answer children's questions all day long, but when attention can be given to the child's question the child should receive the satisfaction of a thoughtful and attentive answer.

Parents should admit their own limitations in thinking and

if necessary should admit their errors and inconsistencies. Too often parents are afraid that they will lose the respect of their children if they admit any errors or limitations in their thinking. On the contrary, if parents will be natural with children with regard to their own thinking, children will then realize that their own verbal efforts are not unlike those of their parents and they will be encouraged to try to approach problems thoughtfully as their parents do. Rather than losing the respect of their children by admitting errors, parents actually help children to appraise them more realistically.

Children should not be forced to find reasons for all of their actions. To demand explanations encourages rationalization and chicanery. Children should be free to think without undue pressure, and parents should avoid distorting the thinking of their children by making unreasonable demands upon them.

Ego development can be aided by relieving children from the threat of punishment. Punishment, or the threat of it, is one of the prime conditions for the arousal of anxiety. Anxiety, if it becomes at all intense, puts pressure on the growing ego to mitigate it and to build up defenses against it. The ego should be free to meet problems in the real world rather than to have to divert some of its energy to protecting itself from threats made against it. Parents, therefore, in the interest of ego development, should use positive methods of freedom and encouragement so far as possible and should avoid the threats arising from punishment.

Education in the Development of the Self

The development of the self is equally important to the development of the ego. It has been pointed out that effective ego development is in part conditioned by the adequate perception and conception of the self. Other things being equal the more self-confidence and self-esteem a child possesses the

more effective will be his learning and his adjustment. Therefore, education must be concerned with helping children to
form positive and constructive self feelings and self evaluations.

The discussion of the social development of the self in
earlier chapters has already hinted at steps which education
must take in order to secure healthy self-esteem. Parents and
teachers should be extremely sensitive to the attitudes they
express toward children, just as children are sensitive to the
attitudes expressed about them. It is important that children
be referred to with warmth, appreciation, encouragement,
and confidence, rather than with criticism, disparagement,
and disappointment. Children respond not only to what is
said to them and about them but also to the attitudes, gestures,
and subtle shades of expression that indicate how parents
and teachers feel. Indeed, these more subtle expressions of
feeling may be taken by the child as representing the parent's
true attitude toward him.

This is not to say a parent should never show disappointment or criticism. Isolated expressions by a parent must be
taken in terms of a larger context. If a child is criticized it
may mean that the parent thinks he is worthless, but it may
also mean that the parent thinks he is worth criticizing because he has greater potentialities than he is now expressing.

Parents have great influence in helping children to form
self-ideals and in helping these ideals become translated into
action. Countless biographies provide illustrations of how the
seeds of greatness in men were planted in childhood by
mothers who had certain ideals and aspirations for their sons,
whispered these ideals and goals in their ears without forcing
them upon them. The fact that concepts of the self are a
reflection of the attitudes expressed toward a person by others
indicates the power that parents and teachers have in determining the kind of selves that children will develop.

Children should be encouraged to adopt a realistic conception and attitude toward themselves. Learning to accept one's own limitations as well as to appreciate one's assets is an important step in self development and will make ego functioning more realistic. Accepting one's limitations in the sense of humbling oneself unnecessarily and belittling oneself becomes a defense mechanism only when the individual finds it necessary to defend himself in this way against attacks (72). Naturally parents should not belittle the child or put unusual demands on him which will necessitate self-belittlement as a defensive measure. Accepting one's limitations can be constructive when it is done realistically.

BIBLIOGRAPHY

1. AICHHORN, August, *Wayward Youth.* New York: The Viking Press, 1925, 1935.

There are two important chapters in this book, one on "The Meaning of the Reality Principle in Social Behavior" and the other, "The Significance of the Ego-Ideal in Social Behavior," both of which discuss the ego of the delinquent from the point of view of factors which lead to delinquency and factors in the treatment of delinquency.

2. AIDMAN, Ted., "Changes in Self Perception as Related to Changes in Perception of One's Environment." *American Psychologist* 3: 286, 1948.

This is an abstract of a paper read at a meeting of the American Psychological Association in which the author presents additional evidence showing that the changes in perception of the self are related to changes in perception of the environment.

3. ALEXANDER, Franz, *Psychoanalysis of the Total Personality.* Nervous and Mental Disease Monograph Series, No. 52. New York: Nervous and Mental Disease Publishing Company, 1929.

In this monograph the author discusses the place of the ego with reference to the various structural divisions of the personality. In particular, he discusses the conflict between the id, the ego, and the superego, and the function of the ego in the integration of these conflicting tendencies.

4. ————, "Development of the Ego-Psychology." In Sandor Lorand, editor, *Psychoanalysis Today.* New York: Covici-Friede, 1933; London: George Allen & Unwin, 1933. Revised and republished, New York: International Universities Press, 1944.

In this chapter Alexander reviews historically the development of the ego in Freudian psychology and indicates that at the present time it occupies a position of central importance.

5. ————, *Fundamentals of Psychoanalysis.* New York: W. W. Norton & Company, 1948.

Chapter V in this book deals with "The Functions of the Ego and its Failures." There is a considerable section dealing with the ego defences.

6. ————, "What is a Neurosis?" *Digest of Neurology and Psychiatry* 16: 225–233, 1948.

This paper, which is a preview of what Alexander included in his later book, *Fundamentals of Psychoanalysis,* is a very clear discussion of the nature of neurosis. In it he likens the ego to a form of government which may be either democratic or autocratic according to whether the ego does or does not recognize all of the many forces which deserve a voice in determining the destiny of the individual. Alexander also emphasizes the relativity of neurosis to the cultural climate in which the individual lives.

7. ———, and FRENCH, T. M., *Psychoanalytic Therapy.* New York: The Ronald Press, 1946.

In this book dealing with procedures in short-term therapy based on psychoanalytic processes, much of the work described is in terms of modifying and strengthening the ego.

8. ALLPORT, G. W., "The Ego in Contemporary Psychology." *Psychological Review* 50: 451–478, 1943.

This presidential address delivered at the annual meeting of the Eastern Psychological Association delivers the ego from its limbo of obscurity and elevates it to a respectable position. Allport lists a number of meanings that may be given to the ego and then proceeds to indicate how the ego plays a rôle of central importance in the psychology of personality. This paper has had considerable influence in dignifying the ego and making it a reputable topic for American psychology.

9. ———, "Effect: A Secondary Principle of Learning." *Psychological Review* 53: 335–347, 1946.

This is the concluding paper in a symposium on "The Law of Effect," in which Allport again presents his belief that the law of effect fails as an explanation of learning when the highly integrated ego is involved.

10. ———, "Personality, a Symposium. III. Geneticism versus Ego-Structure in Theories of Personality." *British Journal of Educational Psychology* 16: 57–68, 1946.

In this symposium, Allport argues that personality is more a function of development than of instinct. He elaborates again his theory of functional autonomy, which states in brief that motives as well as habits and skills have a continuous development throughout life.

11. ALPER, J. G., "Task-Orientation vs. Ego-Orientation in Learning and Retention." *American Journal of Psychology* 59: 236–248, 1946.

This experimental study shows how self-involvement affects learning and retention.

12. ANDERSON, H. H., and BRANDT, H. T., "Study of Motivation Involving Self-Announced Goals of Fifth-Grade Children and the Concept of 'Level of Aspiration.'" *Journal of Social Psychology* 10: 209–232, 1932.

This study shows that children who have been told that their performance is above or below the class average tend to set their goals in the direction of the class average.

13. Bain, Read, "The Self-and-Other Words of a Child." *American Journal of Sociology* 41: 767–775, 1936.

This study by Read Bain repeats an older study by Cooley and confirms many of Cooley's findings with regard to the use of pronouns in the first person by young children. Bain also discusses the significance of language for the development of the self.

14. Baldwin, J. M., *Mental Development in the Child and in the Race,* 3rd ed. New York: The Macmillan Company, 1895, 1903, 1906.

15. ———, *Social and Ethical Interpretations in Mental Development,* 4th ed. New York: The Macmillan Company, 1897, 1902, 1906.

Baldwin, a social psychologist, writing at the opening of the century, devoted considerable attention to the development of the self and was one of the first to stress the social determinants of the self.

16. Balint, Michael, "Ego Strength and Education of the Ego. *Psychoanalytic Quarterly* 11: 87–95, 1942.

This is an important paper clarifying the concept of ego strength and relating it to some factors in the development of the ego. The author suggests the need for a sound program of education designed to assist in strengthening the ego.

17. Benedek, Therese, "Adaptation to Reality in Early Infancy." *Psychoanalytic Quarterly* 7: 200–215, 1938.

In this insightful article, Benedek has proposed the concept of "confidence" as a principle which has a strong influence in ego development. Benedek believes that the infant who has not been disappointed by neglect or harsh treatment by parents develops a sense of confidence which permits attention to be given to stimuli in the outside world and the development of adjustment to outer conditions. The infant without this confidence factor is unable to tolerate deprivation and fails to develop stability of response.

18. Bergler, Edmund, "On the Psychoanalysis of the Ability to Wait and of Impatience." *Psychoanalytic Review* 26: 11–32, 1939.

In this paper an aspect of ego development is discussed relating to the ability to wait and to postpone immediate gratification of impulses.

19. Bernfeld, Siegfried, *Psychology of the Infant.* London: Kegan Paul, 1929; New York: Brentano's, 1929. First published in German under the title, *Psychologie des sainglings,* 1925.

Bernfeld discusses the origin of the ego in the infant and places considerable importance on the development of the grasping reflex and the discrimination by the infant between his own body and other persons and objects.

20. Bertocci, P. A., "The Psychological Self, the Ego and Personality." *Psychological Review* 52: 91–99, 1945.

Bertocci, following Allport, makes a fresh attempt to define the ego as that portion of personality with which the self has identified its greatest value. The ego therefore becomes the nucleus and principal value of the self.

21. BETTELHEIM, Bruno, "Individual and Mass Behavior in Extreme Situations." *Journal of Abnormal and Social Psychology* 38: 417–452, 1943.

This paper discusses the breakdown of the ego under conditions of extreme provocation in two Nazi concentration camps at Dachau and at Buchenwald.

22. BLANCHARD, Phyllis, "Psychoanalytic Contributions to the Problems of Reading Disabilities." *The Psychoanalytic Study of the Child,* Vol. II., pp. 163–187. New York: International Universities Press, 1946.

23. BLOS, Peter, *The Adolescent Personality.* New York: Appleton-Century-Crofts, Inc., 1941.

24. BRENMAN, Margaret, GILL, M. M., and HACKER, F. J., "Alterations in the State of the Ego in Hypnosis." *Bulletin of the Menninger Clinic* 11: 60–66, 1947.

In this short paper the authors summarize their observations concerning modifications of the ego under hypnosis. In general, hypnosis reduces the inhibitory functions of the ego with consequent alterations in perception, thinking, and motor response.

25. BRIERLEY, Marjorie, "Affects in Theory and Practice." *International Journal of Psychoanalysis* 18: 256–268, 1937.

In this paper the part that anxiety and guilt play in the organization of the ego is discussed together with some implications for psychotherapeutic practice.

26. ———, "Notes on Psychoanalysis and Integrative Living." *International Journal of Psychoanalysis* 28: 57–105, 1947.

Here is a fundamental essay attempting to deal with problems of religion and ethics over against the findings of psychoanalysis. The main thesis of the paper is that integrative living requires a more adequate comprehension of the world in which we live and in particular the understanding of the inner world of personality.

27. BRUNER, J. S., and GOODMAN, C. C., "Value and Need as Organizing Factors in Perception." *Journal of Abnormal and Social Psychology* 42: 33–42, 1947.

Bruner's studies on the nature of perception have been little short of revolutionary. They have demonstrated that value and need influence our perception, and that the precise organization of material as perceived is determined by the needs of the individual and the values which he finds in the perception.

28. ———, and POSTMAN, Leo, "Symbolic Value as an Organizing Factor in Perception." *Journal of Social Psychology* 27: 203–208, 1948.

This is a report on later studies concerning motivation as a factor in determining perception.

29. BUCHENHOLZ, Bruce, and FRANK, Richard, "The 'Concept of the Self' in Acute Traumatic Neuroses of War." *Journal of Nervous and Mental Disease* 107: 55–61, 1948.

These authors who had the opportunity of studying acute traumatic war neuroses believe that it is sufficient to reëstablish confidence in the self to enable a person to function again in a satisfactory manner.

30. BYCHOWSKI, Gustav, "The Ego of Homosexuals." *International Journal of Psychoanalysis* 26: 114–127, 1945.

Bychowski believes that the homosexual has never achieved separation from the mother nor has he learned to enter into the society of men. The homosexual is highly narcissistic and is very sensitive to attacks upon the self.

31. CALKINS, M. W., *The Persistent Problems of Philosophy*. New York: The Macmillan Company, 1907, 1917, 1925.

This philosopher-psychologist has taken up the problems of the self in considerable detail as they have been treated by such philosophers as Hume, Kant, Schopenhauer and some of the more modern schools of thought.

32. ———, *A First Book in Psychology*. New York: The Macmillan Company, 4th ed. 1909, 1910, 1912, 1914.

33. ———, "The Self in Scientific Psychology." *American Journal of Psychology* 26: 495–524, 1915.

This distinguished psychologist of a generation ago made a plea for consideration of the self as a protest against the extremely attenuated psychological theories in vogue at that time.

34. CHAPMAN, D. W., and VOLKMANN, J., "A Social Determinant of the Level of Aspiration." *Journal of Abnormal and Social Psychology* 34: 225–238, 1939.

This study presents some rather inconclusive findings with regard to the influence on level of aspiration of a knowledge of the performance of other groups.

35. CHEIN, Isidor, "The Awareness of Self and the Structure of the Ego." *Psychological Review* 51: 309–314, 1944.

This paper was stimulated by the earlier paper on the ego by Allport. Chein proposes a theory that the ego is a structured set of interrelated motives centering about the awareness of self. The point is emphasized that in its origin the ego represents a number of separate behavioral trends.

36. CLARK, L. P., "A Contribution to the Early Development of the Ego." *American Journal of Psychiatry* 11: 1161–1180, 1932.

The discussion in this paper of ego development is based on observations by a psychiatrist of the regression of an individual to stuporous conditions which he believes to be similar to primitive states in ego development.

37. COMBS, A. W., "Phenomenological Concepts in Non-Directive Therapy." *Journal of Consulting Psychology* 12: 197–208, 1948.

An excellent paper paralleling the discussion in the book by Snygg and Combs.

38. COMBS, A. W., "A Phenomenological Approach to Adjustment Theory." *Journal of Abnormal and Social Psychology* 44: 29–35, 1949.

This paper is a fine elaboration of the phenomenological point of view that adjustment depends primarily upon the individual's concept of himself.

39. COOLEY, C. H., *Human Nature and the Social Order*. New York: Charles Scribner's Sons, 1902, 1922.

This book by another social psychologist of a generation ago discusses the development of the self and stresses the social determinants of the self.

40. ———, "A Study of the Early Use of Self-Words by a Child." *Psychological Review* 15: 339–357, 1908.

This early study by a distinguished sociologist grew out of the late G. Stanley Hall era of child study and represents one of the few surveys of the development of the use of personal pronouns by young children.

41. CORIAT, Isador, "The Structure of the Ego." *Psychoanalytic Quarterly* 9: 380–393, 1940.

Coriat makes some basic propositions with regard to the function and organization of the ego and also the function of the ego in the various pathologies.

42. DARWIN, Charles, "Biographical Sketch of an Infant." *Mind* 2: 285–294, 1877.

In this interesting paper Darwin draws upon certain diary material to discuss trends in infant development. There is an interesting passage showing that in early infancy a baby does not recognize the self when he sees his image in a mirror but that this self-reference is something that comes at a later age.

43. DE GROOT, J. L., "On the Development of the Ego and Superego." *International Journal of Psychoanalysis* 28: 7–11, 1947.

This is a very helpful, straightforward statement with regard to the development of the ego, showing some of the relationships between the development of ego processes and self-evaluative tendencies.

44. DEMBO, T., "Der Ärger als Dynamisches Problem (Untersuchungen zur Handlungs und Affektpsychologie X. Edited by Kurt Lewin). *Psychologische Forschung* 15: 1–144, 1931.

In Dembo's study of anger occurs the first use of the term "level of aspiration."

45. DOOLEY, Lucille, "The Concept of Time in Defense of Ego Integrity." *Psychiatry* 4: 13–23, 1941.

Dooley elaborates the significance of time in helping to build the continuity and hence integrity of the ego.

46. DUNLAP, Knight, *A System of Psychology*. New York: Charles Scribner's Sons, 1912.

Chapter 20 of this book is devoted to a brief discussion of the ego which Dunlap relates to his discussion of consciousness.

47. ———, "The Self and the Ego." *Psychological Review* 21: 62–69, 1914.

In this article Dunlap uses the terms *ego* and *self* very much as they are used in this book. However, the ego as Dunlap conceives it is merely the observer and is related to the phenomenon of consciousness. Dunlap does not include the thinking and acting sides of the individual within his concept of the ego.

48. EISENDERFER, Arnold, "Ego Status in Psychoanalysis." *Psychiatric Quarterly* 8: 515–524, 1934.

This author presents an evaluation of ego status necessary as a prerequisite to psychoanalysis. He believes not only that there must be a certain ego structure in order that a psychoanalysis be effective at all, but also that psychoanalysis aids in strengthening the ego and helping it in its synthetic functioning.

49. ENGLISH, O. S., and PEARSON, G. H. J., *Common Neuroses of Children and Adults.* New York: W. W. Norton & Company, 1937.

In this handbook of children's problems the part that the ego plays in neurotic difficulties is given proper prominence.

50. ERIKSON, E. H., "Ego Development and Historical Change." In *The Psychoanalytic Study of the Child,* Vol. II., pp. 359–376. New York: International Universities Press, 1947.

In this interesting paper Erikson discusses ego development in various Indian tribes and in various individuals who have been uprooted from their early conditions of living whom he has had the opportunity of studying intensively. Erikson points out relations between shifting social conditions and the integration of the ego.

51. ESCALONA, S. K., *An Application of the Level of Aspiration Experiment to the Study of Personality.* New York: Contributions to Education No. 937, Teachers College, Columbia University, 1948.

52. FEDERN, Paul, "Some Variations in Ego-Feeling." *International Journal of Psychoanalysis* 7: 434–444, 1926.

This paper discusses body-feelings and self-feelings, their development and regression. There is a discussion of the lack of self-feeling in states of depersonalization and depression. Federn makes comparisons between the feeling tone in waking and dream states.

53. ———, "Narcissism in the Structure of the Ego." *International Journal of Psychoanalysis* 9: 401–419, 1928.

Federn believes that relationships to people depend upon a certain sense of self. The way in which an individual reacts to himself determines to a measure his reactions to other persons. This paper anticipates by two decades the conclusions reached by Sheerer and Stock.

54. FEDERN, Paul, "Ego Feeling in Dreams." *Psychoanalytic Quarterly* 1: 511–542, 1932.

55. ———, "The Awakening of the Ego in Dreams." *International Journal of Psychoanalysis* 15: 296–301, 1934.

In these last two papers, Federn elaborates on his observations on self-feeling in dreams in comparison with the waking state.

56. FENICHEL, Otto, "Ego Disturbances and Their Treatment." *International Journal of Psychoanalysis* 19: 416–438, 1938.

In this paper Fenichel elaborates his point of view that in the psychotherapy of ego or character disturbances it is necessary to change the latent conflicts into current ones. This is not done by reactivating conflicts by fresh traumas but by mobilizing the latent conflicts as they may be observed in small symptoms by ordinary therapeutic means.

57. ———, "The Counter-Phobic Attitude." *International Journal of Psychoanalysis* 20: 263–277, 1939.

58. ———, "The Ego and the Affects." *Psychoanalytic Review* 28: 47–60, 1941.

This is an important paper in which the part the ego plays in such emotional states as anxiety, guilt, shame, etc., is thoroughly discussed.

59. ———, *Psychoanalytical Theory of the Neuroses.* New York: W. W. Norton & Company, 1945.

This compendium of psychoanalytical theory is perhaps the one single most important reference with regard to the development of the ego. In one section Fenichel makes an important analysis of the growth of various mental processes which contribute to ego formation in the infant and draws the clearest picture available in the literature of the growing development of the ego and awareness of the self. In other parts of the book there are discussions of the part that the ego plays in countercathexis or efforts on the part of the individual to repress and hide unacceptable tendencies. There is a fine discussion of the part that the ego plays in structural conflicts. The concept of the ego is used to discuss character formation and anomalies of character.

60. FERENCZI, Sandor, "Steps in the Development of the Sense of Reality." Chapter VIII in *Sex and Psychoanalysis. Contributions to Psychoanalysis.* Boston: Richard G. Badger, 1916. pp. 213–239.

This is one of those choice original papers which serve as a basis for much later thinking in this area. It discusses the growth of the sense of reality with considerable insight and with clarity of expression.

61. ———, "Thinking and Muscle Innervation." *Further Contributions to the Theory and Technique of Psychoanalysis,* Chapter XVIII, pp. 230–232. International Psychoanalytical Library, No. 11. London: The Hogarth Press, 1926; New York: Boni and Liveright, 1927.

In this brief paper Ferenczi anticipates the behaviorist point of view that thinking is implicit action, and by equating thinking with action contributes toward a theory of ego development.

62. ————, "The Problem of the Acceptance of Unpleasant Ideas." *Further Contributions to the Theory and Technique of Psychoanalysis,* Chapter LXXIII, pp. 366–379. International Psychoanalytical Library, No. 11. London: The Hogarth Press, 1926; New York: Boni and Liveright, 1927.

This is a second insightful paper by Ferenczi, in which he introduces the rôle of the ego in the defensive and repressive process.

63. FISHER, M. S., *Language Patterns of Preschool Children.* New York: Bureau of Publications, Teachers College, Columbia University, 1934.

This is Mrs. Mary Shattuck Fisher Langmuir's doctoral dissertation, in which she presents data concerning the language development of young children. Apparently children only use the first person plural pronouns on the average after the third year.

64. FLUGEL, J. C., "A Case of Affective Inhibition of an Intellectual Process." *International Journal of Psychoanalysis* 4: 111–117, 1923.

Although this is the report of a case, there are some significant comments with regard to intellectual inhibition.

65. FODOR, Nandor, *The Search for the Beloved. A Clinical Investigation of the Trauma of Birth and of Pre-Natal Conditioning.* New York: Hermitage Press Inc., 1949.

This book is somewhat on the fringe of reputability. Its author would not hesitate to admit that he has indulged in considerable speculation and that he is far from satisfying the demands of science. To be more precise, Fodor believes that many of an individual's dreams, fantasies, and behavioral tendencies have their origin from the trauma of birth and that even some of the prenatal experiences will influence mental life after birth.

66. FORDHAM, Michael, "Integration and Disintegration and Early Ego Development." *Nervous Child* 6: 266–277, 1947.

Fordham discusses the ego and the self from the point of view of Jung, but his differentiation between these two concepts is not entirely clear.

67. FRANK, J. D., "Individual Differences in Certain Aspects of the Level of Aspiration." *American Journal of Psychology* 47: 119–129, 1935.

In this paper Frank presents evidence to indicate that the level of aspiration is a relatively permanent characteristic of personality.

68. ————, "Some Psychological Determinants of the Level of Aspiration." *American Journal of Psychology* 47: 285–293, 1935.

Frank produces evidence to indicate that the level of aspiration is self-involved either to avoid failure or to keep aspiration high.

69. ————, "The Influence of the Level of Performance in One Task on the Level of Aspiration in Another." *Journal of Experimental Psychology* 18: 159–171, 1935.

70. FRANK, J. D., "Recent Studies of the Level of Aspiration." *Psychological Bulletin* 38: 218–225, 1941.

This is a good review of experimental studies of the level of aspiration which were available to the reviewer a decade ago.

71. FRENCH, T. M., "Reality and the Unconscious." *Psychoanalytic Quarterly* 6: 23–61, 1937.

French has added significantly to the literature on the ego. In this first paper he discusses the relation between adaptation to reality and conscious awareness, and assumes that the two are not necessarily coincident. Individuals can develop in reality adaptation without the coöperation of full consciousness at every step.

72. ———, "Defense and Synthesis in the Function of the Ego." *Psychoanalytic Quarterly* 7: 537–553, 1938.

This paper is a review of Anna Freud's book, *Ego and the Mechanisms of Defense*. While no new points of view are developed, French does emphasize that in its defensive functions the ego is striving to reach a synthesis.

73. ———, "Goal, Medium and Integrative Field." *Psychosomatic Medicine* 3: 226–252, 1941.

French discusses the relation between an individual's goals and his capacity for integration. He believes that the extent to which an individual can achieve his goals is directly a function of the individual's integrative capacity.

74. ———, "Some Psychoanalytic Applications of the Psychological Field Concept." *Psychoanalytic Quarterly* 11: 17–32, 1942.

In this paper French discusses the integrative functions of the ego.

75. ———, "Ego Analysis as a Guide to Therapy." *Psychoanalytic Quarterly* 14: 336–349, 1945.

French defines the basic problem in therapy as that of understanding the ego's integrative task, by which he means to discover the nature of repressed wishes and the defenses raised against them.

76. FRENKEL-BRUNSWIK, Else, "Mechanisms of Self-Deception." *Journal of Social Psychology* 10: 409–420, 1939.

In this paper the author presents data to indicate various mechanisms by which an individual attempts to disguise his true self.

77. FREUD, Anna, *The Ego and the Mechanisms of Defense*. International Psychoanalytical Library, No. 30. London: The Hogarth Press, 1937. (First published in German in 1936.) New York: International Universities Press, 1946.

This is one of the most important contributions in the literature on the ego. For the first time in detail there is set forth the concept that the individual is responsible for his method of defense against anxiety.

78. ———, "Indications for Child Analysis." in *The Psychoanalytic*

Study of the Child, Vol. I. New York: International Universities Press, 1945, pp. 127–149.

While not implied in the title, this paper contains an excellent survey of the steps in ego development from infancy on through the latency period into puberty.

79. FREUD, Sigmund, "Formulations Regarding the Two Principles in Mental Functioning." *Collected Papers,* IV, International Psychoanalytical Library, No. 10. London: The Hogarth Press, 1925, pp. 13–21. (First published in German in 1911.)

This paper of Freud's contrasts the pleasure principle with the reality principle, and with regard to the latter makes significant points with respect to ego development.

80. ———, "On Narcissism: An Introduction." *Collected Papers,* IV, International Psychoanalytical Library, No. 10. London: The Hogarth Press, 1925, pp. 30–59. (First published in German in 1914.)

In this paper Freud points out that ego grows out of primary narcissism and ego development must always represent a development of narcissistic tendencies.

81. ———, *Beyond the Pleasure Principle.* International Psychoanalytical Library, No. 4. London: The Hogarth Press, 1922; New York: Boni and Liveright, 1924. (First published in German in 1920.)

In this brief monograph Freud elaborates on the "reality principle" which serves as a basis for his later discussion of the concept of the ego and its place in personality development.

82. ———, *Group Psychology and the Analysis of the Ego.* International Psychoanalytical Library, No. 6. London: The Hogarth Press, 1922. (First published in German in 1921.)

In this book Freud discusses the place of identification in the formation of the ego. There is also a chapter on the ego-ideal and its relation to the ego.

83. ———, *The Ego and the Id.* International Psychoanalytical Library, No. 12. London: The Hogarth Press, 1927. (First published in German, 1923.)

This compact monograph presents Freud's theories with regard to the structure of personality. It has served as a stimulus to considerable theorizing and speculation and serves as the groundwork for much of the present-day theory with regard to ego development. In one chapter Freud launches his concept of the superego.

84. ———, "Negation." *International Journal of Psychoanalysis* 6: 367–371, 1925.

This short paper makes the point that when a person denies something it is tantamount evidence that the very thing that he denies is implicitly an impulse within him. This paper fortifies the point of view that the ego is the principal determining factor in repression.

85. FREUD, Sigmund, *New Introductory Lectures in Psychoanalysis*. International Psychoanalytical Library, No. 24. London: The Hogarth Press, 1933; New York: W. W. Norton & Company, Inc., 1933.

In this last collection of theoretical papers on psychoanalytical theory Freud reformulates his beliefs concerning the part that the ego plays in defense against anxiety and the conflicts that may take place within the various structures of which a personality is composed.

86. ———, *Inhibitions, Symptoms and Anxiety*. International Psychoanalytical Library, No. 28. London: The Hogarth Press, 1936. First published in English by the Psychoanalytic Institute, Monograph Series No. 8. Stamford, Connecticut, 1927. Published in the United States under the title, *The Problem of Anxiety*. New York: W. W. Norton & Company, Inc., 1936. (First published in German in 1926.)

87. ———, "An Outline of Psychoanalysis." *International Journal of Psychoanalysis* 21: 27–84, 1940.

This compact outline presents a few new points of view with regard to the ego and in particular Freud's position with regard to the splitting of the ego as a result of repression.

88. ———, "Splitting of the Ego in the Defensive Process." *International Journal of Psychoanalysis* 22: 65–68, 1941.

Freud believes that in the defensive process the ego may become split and serve both the repressed and the repressing tendencies.

89. FRIES, M. E., "The Child's Ego Development and the Training of Adults in His Environment." In *The Psychoanalytic Study of the Child*, Vol. II, pp. 85–112. New York: International Universities Press, 1947.

This is a splendid statement of factors conditioning an infant's ego development with an emphasis on the necessity for stable and well-adjusted parents for the most advantageous ego development.

90. GALDSTON, Iago, "On the Etiology of Depersonalization." *Journal of Nervous and Mental Disease* 105: 25–39, 1947.

This paper includes a good review of previous work. The author also presents his own formulation of ego formation in terms of the relation between the id and the superego. He discusses personalization as well as depersonalization, which he believes to be a matter of learning.

91. GARDNER, J. W., "The Use of the Term 'Level of Aspiration.'" *Psychological Review* 47: 59–68, 1947.

Gardner reviews earlier studies, in particular that of Gould in which she concludes that measures used in level of aspiration experiments do not fully represent the level of aspiration of the individual. Gardner, however, takes the point of view that for scientific purposes it is important to restrict the use of the term to those phenomena which can be measured.

92. GATES, A. I., JERSILD, A. T., McCONNELL, T. R. and CHALLMAN, R. C., *Educational Psychology.* New York: The Macmillan Company, 1942. Third edition, 1948.

The section on the level of aspiration in this book is a succinct summary of experimental findings in this area.

93. GILL, M. M., and BRENMAN, Margaret, "Treatment of a Case of Anxiety Hysteria by an Hypnotic Technique Employing Psychoanalytic Principles." *Bulletin of the Menninger Clinic* 7: 163–171, 1943.

These authors discuss the value of a temporary suspension of the ego during hypnosis for psychotherapeutic purposes, also how the material revealed under hypnosis can be integrated into the ego in the normal state.

94. GLOVER, Edward. "Grades of Ego-Differentiation." *International Journal of Psychoanalysis* 11: 1–11, 1930.

Glover points out that the ego arises originally from various nuclei of behavior and points out the various ways in which the ego differentiates to make up the levels of personality structure.

95. ———, "The Concept of Dissociation." *International Journal of Psychoanalysis* 24: 7–13, 1943.

Glover analyzes dissociation from the point of view of the differentiation of the ego.

96. GLOVER, James, "The Conception of the Ego." *International Journal of Psychoanalysis* 7: 414–419, 1926.

Although this paper is two decades old, it is remarkable for the insight shown and the clarity of expression. Most of the present-day points of view with regard to the ego were anticipated in this paper.

97. GOODENOUGH, F. L., "The Use of Pronouns by Young Children: A Note on the Development of Self-Awareness." *Journal of Genetic Psychology* 52: 333–346, 1938.

This is another paper on the development of the use of first person pronouns and their relation to the growth of the ego.

98. GOULD, Rosalind, "Factors Underlying Expressed 'Level of Aspiration.'" *Journal of Psychology* 6: 265–279, 1938.

This paper, which is a discussion of her doctoral study published in the Genetic Psychology Monographs, is a very insightful paper which shows that level of aspiration cannot be thought of simply in terms of the measures which are used experimentally in its study, but that the individual's own feelings must be taken into account.

99. ———, "An Experimental Analysis of 'Level of Aspiration.'" *Genetic Psychology Monographs* 21: 3–115, 1939.

This doctoral dissertation is noteworthy because, in addition to obtaining experimental findings, the author interviews each subject to find out how he reacts to success or failure and finds that a given relation between level of aspiration and performance may be interpreted in quite different ways by different subjects.

100. GUTHEIL, Emil, "Depersonalization." *Psychoanalytic Review* 17: 26–54, 1930.

Gutheil presents conclusions from cases of depersonalization which have come under his observations which corroborate the findings of other investigators.

101. GUTHRIE, E. R., and EDWARDS, A. L., *Psychology.* New York: Harper and Brothers, 1949.

These authors, in attempting to be behavioristic, still avoid the term "unconscious" and speak of verbal and non-verbal attitudes toward the self. Their discussion of the self is limited and inadequate.

102. HAIGH, Gerard, "Defensive Behavior in Client-Centered Therapy." *Journal of Consulting Psychology* 13: 181–189, 1949.

This study attempts to measure defensive behavior from the analysis of counseling protocols, but naturally the signs of defensiveness studied are limited to those which show themselves in verbal expression by the client, and this markedly constricts the value of the study.

103. HARMS, Ernest, "Ego-Inflation and Ego-Deflation." *The Nervous Child* 6: 284–300, 1947.

The author discusses the important concepts of self-inflation and self-deflation, but the article is not as helpful as it might be, partly because of the inadequate theoretical background and partly because of rambling and loose organization.

104. HART, H. H., "Narcissistic Equilibrium." *International Journal of Psychoanalysis* 28: 106–114, 1947.

In this paper Hart discusses the problem of values of different types of narcissism. It is well known that in some instances narcissism is an asset and signifies individual stability and well-being, while in other instances narcissism represents a fantasy appraisal of the self. Hart recognizes different levels of integration of narcissistic tendencies with the ego structure and believes that the most wholesome condition is one in which narcissistic tendencies are thoroughly integrated with ego and superego tendencies.

105. HARTMANN, Heinz, "Ich-Psychologie und Anpassungsproblem." *Internationale Zeitschrift für Psychoanalyze und Imago* 24: 62–135, 1939.

This article by a leading psychoanalyst has long been recognized as a fundamental contribution to the literature on the basis of ego development and its synthetic functions.

106. ———, "Psychoanalysis and the Concept of Health." *International Journal of Psychoanalysis* 20: 308–321, 1939.

Hartmann believes that conflicts are "a part and parcel of human development, for which they provide the necessary stimulus." He believes that the mechanisms of defense play a part in determining normal as well as pathological processes.

107. ———, KRIS, Ernst, and LOEWENSTEIN, R. M., "Comments on the Formation of Psychic Structure." In *The Psychoanalytic Study of the Child,* Vol. II, pp. 11–38. New York: International Universities Press, 1947.

This is a somewhat abstract but authoritative statement concerning some of the fundamental principles of ego development in infancy.

108. ———, "On Rational and Irrational Action." In Geza Roheim, editor, *Psychoanalysis and Social Science,* Vol. I. New York: International Universities Press, 1947, pp. 359–392.

The author discusses the relation between rationality and adaptation.

109. HAVIGHURST, R. J., ROBINSON, M. Z., and DORR, Mildred, "The Development of the Ideal Self in Childhood and Adolescence." *Journal of Educational Research* 40: 241–257, 1946.

These authors have asked children about their ideals and find that they tend to idealize in their actual environment people who impress them with their outstanding qualities.

110. HERTZMAN, Max, and FESTINGER, Leon, "Shifts in Explicit Goals in a Level of Aspiration Experiment." *Journal of Experimental Psychology* 27: 439–452, 1940.

The experiment performed by these two investigators indicates that there is a shift in the average difference score between performance and level of aspiration in the direction of the supposed average difference score of the group.

111. HILGARD, E. R., "Human Motives and the Concept of the Self." *American Psychologist* 4: 374–382, 1949.

In this presidential address before the American Psychological Association, Hilgard points out how the self can be a unifying concept in problems of motivation.

112. HOFFER, Willie, "Mouth, Hand and Ego-Integration." In *The Psychoanalytic Study of the Child,* Vol. III/IV, pp. 49–56. New York: International Universities Press, 1949.

This article by Hoffer is mainly concerned with the function of the hand in early infant development and shows how the hand functions to help the infant bridge the gap between his inner experiences and the outer world.

113. HOPPE, Ferdinand, "Erfolg und Misserfolg. Untersuchungen zur Handlungs und Affectpsychologie: XX." (Edited by Kurt Lewin.) *Psychologische Forschung* 14: 1–62, 1930.

This is a report on the first experiment on the level of aspiration.

114. HORNEY, Karen, *New Ways in Psychoanalysis*. New York: W. W. Norton & Company, Inc., 1939.

Quoting William James, Horney reports that her analytic experience leads her to the conclusion that giving up one's pretentions leads to greater relief than gratifying one's aims.

115. HOROWITZ, E. L., "Spatial Localization of the Self." *Journal of Social Psychology* 6: 379–387, 1935.

In this interesting study the author asks children in what part of the body the self is located and presents evidence to show that different children localize the self in different parts of the body.

116. HOROWITZ, Ruth, "Racial Aspects of Self-Identification in Nursery School Children." *Journal of Psychology* 7: 91–99, 1939.

This investigator asked children to identify themselves from pictures of white and Negro children. She concludes that forming a concept of one's social rôle is an important part of forming a concept of the self.

117. HUME, David, *Treatise on Human Nature*. 1739. Book I, Part IV, Everyman's Library Series, No. 548. New York: E. P. Dutton and Company, 1911.

Hume was the first philosopher to make a break in the age-old concept of the soul as a distinct entity.

118. ISAACS, Susan, *Social Development in Young Children*. New York: Harcourt, Brace and Company, 1937.

Mrs. Isaacs introduces the concept of the ego from time to time in this book. She is particularly clear in her analysis of reality testing.

119. JACOBSON, Edith, "The Effect of Disappointment on Ego and Super-ego Formation in Normal and Depressive Development." *Psychoanalytic Review* 33: 129–147, 1946.

Disappointment in childhood leads to a shrinking of the ego and in some cases to an overdevelopment of the superego. Since a child fails to please its parents, he learns to place trust and support in his own ideals and standards.

120. JAMES, William, *Psychology*. New York: Henry Holt and Company, 1890. Vols. 1, 2.

Although written many years ago, James' chapters on the self are still sound reading. He makes the distinction between the self as observed and the self as observer, a distinction which has been kept in the present treatment using the two terms *ego* and *self* to clarify and emphasize the distinction.

121. JUCKNAT, Margarete, "Leistung Anspruchsniveau und Selbstbewusstsein." *Psychologische Forschung* 22: 89–179, 1938.

Among many findings in this comprehensive study is one in which it has been demonstrated that the influence of success or failure in one situation involves the level of aspiration in another situation.

122. JUNG, C. G., *Psychological Types.* New York: Harcourt, Brace and Company, 1923.

Jung defines the ego as the subject of consciousness, whereas the self, which includes the ego, is the subject of one's total personality and includes unconscious as well as conscious tendencies.

123. ——, *Contributions to Analytical Psychology.* London: Kegan Paul, Trench, Trubner and Company, Ltd., 1928.

Jung's statements are never too clear. In this series of essays, he defines the ego as "that unique complex whose inner cohesion means consciousness." He also refers to the "ego complex" which he states forms the center of individuality and is but one of several complexes which have more peripheral rôles.

124. KANT, Immanuel, *Critique of Pure Reason.* 1781, 1787. Everyman's Library Series, No. 909. New York: E. P. Dutton and Company.

Kant is the first to recognize a contrast between a subject self and an object self, a discrimination that forms the basis of the treatment in the present book.

125. KISKER, G. W., and KNOX, G. W., "The Psychopathology of the Ego System." *Journal of Nervous and Mental Disease* 96: 66–71, 1943.

Kisker and Knox have been impressed with the gestalt point of view with regard to ego development developed by Koffka. They discuss various pathological states from the gestalt point of view.

126. KLEIN, G. S., and SCHOENFELD, W. N., "The Influence of Ego-Involvement on Confidence." *Journal of Abnormal and Social Psychology* 36: 249–258, 1941.

In this experimental study it is demonstrated that confidence is either strengthened or weakened to the degree that the task is one in which the self is involved.

127. KLEIN, Melanie, "The Importance of Symbol-Formation in the Development of the Ego." *International Journal of Psychoanalysis* 11: 24–39, 1930.

The author stresses the importance of symbols on the fantasy level for the development of the ego and points out that without this fantasy structure the infant is bereft of methods of testing reality, of developing thinking processes, and of reaching out in the direction of its future development.

128. ——, "A Contribution to the Theory of Intellectual Inhibition." *International Journal of Psychoanalysis* 12: 206–218, 1931.

In this paper the author elaborates the theory that there may be intellectual deterioration as a result of emotional conflicts which would actually result in pseudo feeble-mindedness.

129. ——, *The Psychoanalysis of Children.* International Psychoanalytical Library, No. 22. London: The Hogarth Press, 1932.

In this book there is a good picture of ego development at different stages.

The author describes with particular clarity the attempts made by the ego to master anxiety.

130. KOFFKA, Kurt, *Principles of Gestalt Psychology*. New York: Harcourt, Brace and Company, 1935.

Koffka devotes a long chapter in this book to the ego. He would see the self as a field phenomenon in which various forces play a part and in which various figures take shape.

131. KRIS, W. E., "Ego Development and the Comic." *International Journal of Psychoanalysis* 19: 77–90, 1938.

Kris points out how comic situations are self-involved to the extent that the individual responds to them. The comic is used by an individual to master situations in which he feels threatened or to avoid defeat, but this method of meeting difficulties is not lasting and has to be continually repeated.

132. LAFORGUE, René, "The Ego and the Conception of Reality." *International Journal of Psychoanalysis* 20: 403–407, 1939.

Laforgue is interested in how the ego perceives reality at various stages of development. He tends to equate the development of the ego with a more effective perception of reality.

133. ———, *The Relativity of Reality: Reflections on the Limitations of Thought and the Genesis of the Need for Causality*. Nervous and Mental Disease Monograph Series, No. 66. New York: Nervous and Mental Disease Publishing Company, 1940.

Laforgue is interested in this treatise with a theory of Freud's that the ego has a characteristic structure at various stages of development so that it is possible to speak of the oral ego, the anal ego, and the genital ego. He believes that the child's scientific approach to reality is possible only after the magical stage is passed on the anal level, and the reality and security of relationships with people has been approached and mastered on the last stage of infantile development.

134. LAIRD, John, *Problems of the Self*. New York: The Macmillan Company, 1917.

This philosopher's book on the self has for many years been a classic statement.

135. LECKY, Prescott, *Self-consistency: a Theory of Personality*. New York: Island Press, 1945.

This brief statement has attracted the interest of psychologists because of the emphasis on integration of personality. Lecky believes that there is an inevitable striving toward self-consistency which can be counted on as a constructive influence in any process of psychotherapy.

136. LEWIN, Kurt, "Psychology of Success and Failure." *Occupations* 14: 926–930, 1936.

In this article Lewin attempts to define success and failure in terms of the level of aspiration.

137. ———, DEMBO, Tamara, FESTINGER, Leon, and SEARS, P. S., "Level of Aspiration." In J. McV. Hunt, *Personality and the Behavior Disorders,* Vol. I, Ch. 10, pp. 333–378. New York: The Ronald Press, 1944.

In this chapter one finds the most complete summary of investigations on the level of aspiration together with Lewin's topological analysis of the level of aspiration.

138. ———, and ZEIGARNIK, Bluma, "Untersuchungen zur Handlungs und Affektpsychologie, III; Das Behalternerledigter und Unledigter Handlungen." *Psychologische Forschung* 9: 1–85, 1927.

This is the original study which demonstrates that tasks completed are not remembered as well as tasks uncompleted. More recent studies have indicated that this is a function of self-involvement in the task.

139. LEWIS, H. B., and FRANKLIN, Muriel, "An Experimental Study of the Rôle of the Ego in Work. II. The Significance of Task-Orientation in Work." *Journal of Experimental Psychology* 34: 195–215, 1944.

140. MAHLER, M. S., "Pseudo-Imbecility: A Magic Case of Invincibility." *Psychoanalytic Quarterly* 11: 149–164, 1942.

This study presents cases which illustrate how children may use pseudo-imbecility in order to participate without censure in the sexual life of the parents.

141. ———, "Ego Psychology Applied to Behavior Problems." In N. D. C. Lewis, and B. L. Pacella, *Modern Trends in Child Psychiatry,* pp. 43–56. New York: International Universities Press, 1945.

Mahler discusses some of the factors contributing to ego strength. She finds the concept of ego strength an important tool for the understanding of primary behavior disorders in children. Mahler tends to equate mental health with ego strength.

142. MAYER-GROSS, W., "On Depersonalization." *British Journal of Medical Psychology* 15: 103–126, 1935.

This is a very good paper describing the symptoms of depersonalization. The discussion at the end of the paper is also noteworthy with significant remarks by Searl and Hadfield.

143. McDOUGALL, William, *An Introduction to Social Psychology.* Boston: John W. Luce and Company, 1908.

The self occupies an important place in McDougall's psychology. He refers to the self-regarding sentiments which include self-esteem.

144. McGEHEE, William, "Judgment and the Level of Aspiration." *Journal of General Psychology* 22: 3–15, 1940.

McGehee demonstrates that level of aspiration is not the same as judgment.

He believes that the self is more involved in determining the level of aspiration than in determining a judgment as to one's future performance.

145. MEAD, G. H., *Mind, Self and Society*. Chicago: University of Chicago Press, 1934.

This book by one of America's outstanding philosophers and social psychologists has attracted the attention of serious students. Section 2 deals with the origin of the self. Mead elaborates in considerable detail the relation between a person's awareness of himself in relation to his reactions to other persons. For Mead the self is determined in large measure by the individual's social relations.

146. MOORE, J. S., "The Problem of the Self." *Philosophical Review* 42: 487–499, 1933.

A philosophical discussion of the meanings of the self. Moore starts in with the self as subject and passes from this very intimate meaning to self as object— the body, the mind, and the peripheral connections of the self.

147. MOWRER, O. H., "The Law of Effect and Ego Psychology." *Psychological Review* 53: 321–334, 1946.

This second article in the symposium on the law of effect elaborates on the relations between the ego and the law of effect. Mowrer points out how one responds to inner signs which may be fully as effective as outer satisfying or annoying stimuli.

148. ———, *Learning Theory and Personality Dynamics*. New York: The Ronald Press, 1950.

In a chapter "On the Psychology of Talking Birds—A Contribution to Language and Personality Theory." Mowrer proposes some hypotheses to account for the development of language. He suggests that an infant may adopt language sounds in part to replace within himself the absent mother who uses the same sounds.

149. MURPHY, Gardner, *Personality*. New York: Harper and Brothers, 1947.

Murphy's treatise on personality is an important reference with regard to the psychology of the self. In Section 3 Murphy discusses the origin of the self, modes of self-enhancement, and self-defense. In a later section he elaborates in considerable detail the concept of integration, and finally points out in a concluding section how the self is related to the social group in which it develops.

150. ———, MURPHY, L. B., and NEWCOMB, Theodore, *Experimental Social Psychology*. New York: Harper and Brothers, 1931; revised edition, 1937.

The problem of the development of the self is discussed in several places in this book. These authors, by suitable illustrations, make very clear the way in which an infant learns to separate himself from his surroundings, particularly his mother.

151. NICOLE, J. E., "The Concept of the Ego in Psychiatry, with Special Reference to Psychoanalysis." *Journal of Mental Science* 75: 427–439, 1929.

This paper contains a sound statement of the Freudian point of view with regard to the ego and also reviews later theories of the self.

152. NUNBERG, Herman, "The Synthetic Function of the Ego." *International Journal of Psychoanalysis* 12: 123–140, 1931.

I would consider this one of the most significant of the papers discussing the ego. It stresses the synthetic function of the ego and the tendency for the ego to become unified and organized.

153. ———, "Ego Strength and Ego Weakness." *American Imago* 3, No. 3: 25–40, August 1942.

This paper has helped to define and clarify concepts of ego strength and ego weakness.

154. OBENDORF, C. P., "Depersonalization in Relation to Eroticization of Thought." *International Journal of Psychoanalysis* 15: 271–295, 1934.

This writer has a theory that in certain kinds of cross-sexual identification the thought processes, instead of serving their function of helping the individual to adapt to reality, become eroticized and the individual finds pleasure in thinking for its own sake. Obendorf sees the individual who uses thinking for the attainment of pleasure as representing a degree of depersonalization.

155. ———, "Feelings of Unreality." *Archives of Neurology and Psychiatry* 36: 322–330, 1936.

This writer believes that the feeling of unreality is due to the repression of thinking which has been eroticized through identification with the parent of the opposite sex.

156. ———, "On Retaining the Sense of Reality in States of Depersonalization." *International Journal of Psychoanalysis* 20: 137–147, 1939.

In this paper Obendorf discusses the general impoverishment of the self as an individual turns away from contact with people toward things and ideas.

157. PIAGET, Jean, *The Language and Thought of the Child.* London: Kegan Paul, Trench, Trubner and Company, Ltd.; New York: Harcourt, Brace and Company, 1926.

158. ———, *Judgment and Reasoning in the Child.* London: Kegan Paul, Trench, Trubner and Company, Ltd.; New York: Harcourt Brace and Company, 1928.

159. ———, *The Child's Conception of the World.* London: Kegan Paul, Trench, Trubner and Company, Ltd.; New York: Harcourt, Brace and Company, 1929.

160. ———, *The Child's Conception of Physical Causality.* London:

Kegan Paul, Trench, Trubner and Company, Ltd.; Harcourt, Brace and Company, 1930.

161. PIAGET, Jean, *The Moral Judgment of the Child*. London: Kegan Paul, Trench, Trubner and Company, Ltd., 1932.

Piaget, a Swiss psychologist, has made noteworthy studies of the development of the mind which are reported in these five volumes. The first two volumes have to do with the development of the simpler thought processes. The child's conceptual development is discussed in the third and fourth volumes, and the child's moral evaluations are discussed in the final volume. Piaget has not only made careful observations but has contributed many helpful concepts by which mental development can be described.

162. PIERCE, C. L., "The Objective and Subjective Development of the Ego." *Archives of Psychoanalysis* 1: 1–92, 1926.

This long paper discusses the development of narcissism and various phenomena of ego development at the beginning of life, the material secured from the analysis of adults.

163. PRINCE, Morton, *The Dissociation of a Personality; A Biographical Study in Abnormal Psychology*, 2nd edition. New York: Longmans, Green and Company, 1905, 1913.

Morton Prince has long been accepted as an authority on the split personality.

164. RADO, Sándor, "An Anxious Mother. A Contribution to the Analysis of the Ego." *International Journal of Psychoanalysis* 9: 219–226, 1928.

Using a scene observed on a beach in which a mother is constantly restricting the play of a child, Rado elaborates on a mechanism now known as maternal overprotection, but at the time that he wrote he described it in terms of expressing hate through love and paying a penalty for the expression of hostility.

165. ———, "The Problem of Melancholia." *International Journal of Psychoanalysis* 9: 420–438, 1928.

Rado elaborates still further the mechanism of self-punishment in melancholia whereby the ego submits to being punished by the superego.

166. RAIMY, V. C., *The Self-Concept as a Factor in Counseling and Personality Organization*. Unpublished doctoral thesis. Ohio State University, 1943.

167. ———, "Self-Reference in Counseling Interviews." *Journal of Consulting Psychology* 12: 153–163, 1948.

This is a digest of Raimy's doctoral thesis in which he elaborates the point of view, which he was the first to express, that psychotherapy is a process of changing the concept of the self.

168. RIBBLE, M. A., *The Rights of Infants*. New York: Columbia University Press, 1943.

In this small volume Ribble asserts, without too much confirming evidence, her belief that mental development is conditioned in part by healthy emotional development.

169. RIBOT, Th., *Diseases of Memory; An Essay in Positive Psychology.* London, 1882; New York: D. Appleton & Company, 1882.

Ribot, working long before Freud's discoveries, is aware of the part that the self plays in mental disease and makes clumsy attempts to define mental disturbance in terms of conflicts within the personality.

170. ———, *The Diseases of Personality.* Chicago: Open Court Publishing Company, 1891, 1906.

In this book Ribot elaborates still further his concept of conflict, anticipating roughly some of the pronouncements of Freud and other psychoanalysts.

171. RICE, P. B., "The Ego and the Law of Effect." *Psychological Review* 53: 307–320, 1946.

This first paper in the symposium on the law of effect analyzes and discusses Allport's original position that the law of effect breaks down and fails to explain learning under conditions of self involvement.

172. ROGERS, C. R., *Counseling and Psychotherapy.* Boston: Houghton Mifflin Company, 1942.

173. ———, "Some Observations on the Organization of Personality." *The American Psychologist* 2: 358–368, 1947.

This address by the retiring president of the American Psychological Association describes his observations of changes in personality in terms of changing perceptions of the self. Rogers has perhaps oversimplified the problem to some extent and has failed to give proper weight to the valuation of the self as contrasted with the perception of the self.

174. ———, "A Non-Objective Introduction." *Journal of Consulting Psychology* 13: 149–153, 1949.

This paper is an introduction to a series of experimental papers bearing on psychotherapy. Rogers' own interpretation of the papers which follow helps to clarify them.

175. ROSENZWEIG, Saul. "An Experimental Study of 'Repression' with Special Reference to Need-Persistence and Ego-Defensive Reactions to Frustration." *Journal of Experimental Psychology* 32: 64–74, 1943.

176. SANFORD, R. N., "Dominance Versus Autocracy and the Democratic Character." *Childhood Education* 23: 109–114, November 1946.

Sanford is of the opinion that the democratic social structure leads to fuller ego development than an autocratic social structure.

177. SCHILDER, Paul, *Introduction to a Psychoanalytic Psychiatry.* Nervous and Mental Disease Monographs Series, No. 50. New York: Nervous and Mental Disease Publishing Company, 1928.

In this book, Chapter I deals with the self-ideal; Chapter II with the ego instincts, and Chapter III with the self-ideal and the perceptive self.

178. SCHILDER, Paul, *The Image and Appearance of the Human Body.* Psyche Monograph, No. 6. London: Kegan Paul, Trench, Trubner and Company, 1935.

Schilder, perhaps more than any other writer, has helped us to understand the relation of the self to the body and the part that the body plays in the development of the self at all stages.

179. ———, and WECHSLER, David, "What Do Children Know of the Interior of their Bodies?" *International Journal of Psychoanalysis* 16: 355–360, 1935.

This is a report on a study which made inquiry into children's concepts of the interior of their bodies.

180. SCHMIDEBERG, Melitta, "Knowledge, Thinking and Intuition." *Psychological and Social Series,* Paper 5, 1946.

This insightful article discusses some of the factors involved in the inhibition of thinking. She believes that human beings are far from realizing their maximum capacities in the thoughtful approach to situations.

181. ———, "Methods of Approach to the Infant Mind, a Study of His Ego Activities." *Nervous Child* 6: 278–283, 1947.

This article by Schmideberg presents some of her first-hand observations of the development of mental processes in infancy.

182. SCHÖNBERGER, Stephen, "Disorders of the Ego in Wartime." *British Journal of Medical Psychology* 21: 248–253, 1947–1948.

This author comments on the phenomenon of depersonalization as observed in wartime casualties.

183. SCHOPENHAUER, Arthur, *The Fourfold Root of the Principle of Sufficient Reason.* 1813.

Schopenhauer also discusses the subjective and objective self. He believes that we are able to perceive the self that wills, but not the self that knows.

184. SEARL, Nina, "Danger Situations of the Immature Ego." *International Journal of Psychoanalysis* 10: 423–435, 1929.

This paper by Searl points out the relation of the ego to anxiety, and the groundwork is laid for a discussion of the defensive functions of the ego.

185. ———, "The Rôles of Ego and Libido in Development." *International Journal of Psychoanalysis* 11: 125–149, 1930.

Searl discusses the availability for the ego of free libido not connected with sex for purposes of sublimation.

186. ———, "A Note on Depersonalization." *International Journal of Psychoanalysis* 13: 329–347, 1932.

Searl stresses in this paper the importance of not being loved as a factor in depersonalization.

187. SEARS, P. S., "Levels of Aspiration in Academically Successful and Unsuccessful Children." *Journal of Abnormal and Social Psychology* 35: 498–536, 1940.

Sears has made a noteworthy contribution to the study of level of aspiration by comparing successful and unsuccessful children in school. She believes that self-confident, successful children react to the level of aspiration situation in a similar way, but unsuccessful children, lacking in confidence, may adopt one of a number of behavior techniques in order to protect their self-esteem in the presence of threat.

188. SHEERER, E. T., "An Analysis of the Relationship between Acceptance of and Respect for Self and Acceptance of and Respect for Others in Ten Counseling Cases." *Journal of Consulting Psychology* 13: 169–175, 1949.

This is a report of a study in which a relation is found between acceptance of and respect for the self and acceptance of and respect for other people.

189. SHERIF, Muzafer, *The Psychology of Social Norms*. New York: Harper and Brothers, 1936.

This book attracted considerable attention from social psychologists when published. It discusses the development of the ego as the product of social institutions.

190. ———, "Some Methodological Remarks Related to Experimentation in Social Psychology (Illustrated by a Review of Current Experimental Work in Ego-involvements)." *International Journal of Opinion and Attitude Research* 1 (2): 71–93, 1947.

This is an excellent review of current research regarding self-involvement. It should serve as a satisfactory digest of Sherif and Cantril's book, *The Psychology of Ego-Involvements.*

191. ———, and CANTRIL, Hadley, *The Psychology of Ego Involvements.* New York: John Wiley and Sons, 1947.

This is, next to Fenichel, perhaps the most important discussion of ego development available today. The first chapters are an elaboration of Sherif's decade-old treatise in which the social basis of ego formation is stressed. The ego is discussed as an attitude. There are chapters devoted to the development of the ego at different stages and a very insightful chapter on adolescence. There is also a chapter on ego deterioration. The last chapter in the book is very critical of the psychoanalytic theory of ego structure. Failing to recognize that many of the points made early in the book are derived from Freud's early writings, these writers in their hostility to the psychoanalytic point of view fail to discriminate between the ego and the superego, and consequently lose an opportunity to elaborate on a distinction which has already demonstrated its importance.

192. Snygg, Donald, and Combs, A. W., *Individual Behavior*. New York: Harper and Brothers, 1948.

This is one of the more significant books of the present day in which the authors develop what they call the "phenomenological" point of view. They discuss the phenomenal self, by which they mean the self as the individual experiences it. This term "phenomenal self" is identical with the term "self" as it is used in this book. These authors also use the term, "self concept," by which they mean the core or central value pertaining to the phenomenal self.

193. Spitz, R. A., "Anaclitic Depression." In *The Psychoanalytic Study of the Child*, Vol. II, pp. 313–342. New York: International Universities Press, 1947.

This is an insightful report on the effect on infants in the first year of being deserted by their mothers. Spitz believes that even temporary desertion by mothers has a depressing effect on infant development.

194. Stanback, Oscar, "Arrested Ego Development and its Treatment in Conduct Disorders and Neuroses of Childhood." *Nervous Child* 6: 306–317, 1947.

This paper discusses educative processes needed in ego development. The author points out that the ego does not develop without the necessary conditions and stimulation, and he proposes that parents should be aware of what kinds of experiences help an infant and young child develop ego strength.

195. Sterba, Richard, "The Fate of the Ego in Analytic Therapy." *International Journal of Psychoanalysis* 15: 117–126, 1934.

This helpful paper discusses the transformations of the ego during the process of analyic therapy and the rôle the ego plays at various stages of the process.

196. Stock, Dorothy, "An Investigation into the Interrelations between the Self Concept and Feelings Directed toward Other Persons and Groups." *Journal of Consulting Psychology* 13: 176–180, 1949.

Stock verifies findings by Sheerer and indicates that as an individual becomes more accepting of himself during psychotherapy he also becomes more accepting of others.

197. Symonds, P. M., *The Dynamics of Human Adjustment*. New York: Appleton-Century-Crofts, Inc., 1946.

References to the ego and the self are sprinkled throughout this book. In particular, in the chapter on "Introjection and the Superego," there is a discussion of the relation between the ego and the superego, and in the chapter on "Love and Self-Love" there is an extended discussion of narcissism, both in its normal and pathological phases.

198. ———, "How Do Good Habits of Thinking Begin?" *Childhood Education* 23: 309–314, 1947.

This somewhat popular article discusses some of the educational factors which concern the development of thinking.

199. THORNDIKE, E. L., *The Psychology of Wants, Interests and Attitudes.* New York: D. Appleton-Century Company, Inc., 1935.

Thorndike presents evidence that the law of effect determines the selection and learning of wants, interests, and attitudes as well as motor and verbal learning.

200. TOEMAN, Z., "Clinical Psychodrama: Auxiliary Ego Double and Mirror Techniques." *Sociometry* 9: 178–183, 1946.

This paper discusses the use of psychodrama in the treatment of psychotic patients. In the auxiliary ego double technique both the patient and his auxiliary double are on the stage and both may be acting the same part. In the mirror technique, however, the subject is a member of the audience and his auxiliary ego is on the stage acting the rôle of the patient.

201. TRESSELT, M. E., and LEVY, Bernard, "Recognition for Ego-Involved Material." *Journal of Psychology* 27: 73–78, 1949.

This paper presents evidence to indicate that recognition-memory is a function of the degree of self-involvement in the material which is to be recognized.

202. UPDEGRAFF, R., and KEISTER, M. E., "A Study of Children's Reactions to Failure and an Experimental Attempt to Modify them." Reported in Gardner Murphy, L. B. Murphy, and T. M. Newcomb, *Experimental Social Psychology*, 434 ff. New York: Harper and Brothers, 1931, 1937.

This study indicates that children are able to learn fairly readily modes of reacting to failure. This is in contrast to the conclusions reached from some of the level of aspiration studies, indicating that individuals in general tend to have a rather stable level of aspiration. Apparently reactions to success and failure are more easily molded in childhood than in later life.

203. WAELDER, Robert, "The Psychoanalytic Theory of Play." *Psychoanalytic Quarterly* 2: 208–224, 1933.

This paper on psychoanalytic theory of play is another gem setting forth important principles in a paper that is destined to become classic. Waelder points out that play serves a valuable rôle in reality testing. By testing situations in fantasy the child becomes adjusted to them and is better able to approach difficult and untried situations of a similar kind in reality.

204. WARREN, R. P., *All the King's Men.* New York: Harcourt, Brace and Company, 1946.

205. WINNICOTT, D. W., "Primitive Emotional Development." *International Journal of Psychoanalysis* 26: 139–143, 1945.

This is a very fine paper in which the author points out many elusive factors not heretofore recognized in the beginning of the integration of personality and the formation of the ego.

206. WINNIK, Heintick, "On the Structure of the Depersonalization-Neurosis." *British Journal of Medical Psychology* 21: 268–277, 1947–1948.

This author distinguishes between true depersonalization as a form of neurosis and temporary depersonalization, in which an individual suffers a temporary lapse of personality integration.

207. WITTELS, Fritz, "Psychology and Treatment of Depersonalization." *Psychoanalytic Review* 27: 57–64, 1940.

Wittels sees depersonalization resulting from many of the identifications that an individual has made at various stages in development being condemned by the superego and hence being blotted out of awareness.

208. WOLBERG, L. R., "The Problem of Self-Esteem in Psychotherapy." *New York State Journal of Medicine* 43: 1415–1419, 1943.

209. WOLFF, Werner, "Experimental Self-Analysis." *Ciba Symposia* 7: 1, 2, 1945.

In these two issues of *Ciba Symposia* Wolff reports the results of some experiments which indicate that the conscious evaluation of the self does not always agree with unconscious evaluations.

210. YERKES, R. M., "The Mind of a Gorilla." *Genetic Psychology Monographs* 2: Nos. 1, 2, 1–193, 1927.

This monograph presents Yerkes' experience in studying the primates. There is a brief mention in this monograph of mirror reactions of the gorilla in which Yerkes finds no evidence of self-reference.

211. YOUNG, Kimball, *Personality and Problems of Adjustment.* New York: Appleton-Century-Crofts, Inc., 1940.

In this treatment of adjustment Young devotes a considerable section to the problem of self development, drawing heavily on G. H. Mead's work.

(1)

INDEX

Date Due

2/4/65	NOV 16 1976		
DEC 8 '65	MAY 18 78		
JAN 8 '66			
FEB 2 '66			
MAR 2 '66			
MAR 16 '66			
MAR 30 '66			
APR 13 '66			
MAY 7 '67			
NOV 1 '67			
MAY 15 '68			
JAN 15 '70			
MAY 19			
FEB 2 3 1973 FEB 21 1975			
MAY 2 1 1976			